GERARD CHAI

Mum's Favourite

RECIPES

Presented Through a

Journey in Time

To order additional copies of this book, contact
Toll Free +65 3165 7531 (Singapore)
Toll Free +60 3 3099 4412 (Malaysia)
www.partridgepublishing.com/singapore
orders.singapore@partridgepublishing.com

ISBN
ISBN: 978-1-5437-7275-3 (sc)
ISBN: 978-1-5437-7274-6 (hc)
ISBN: 978-1-5437-7273-9 (e)

Print information available on the last page.

02/14/2023

PARTRIDGE

To my father.

CONTENTS

FOREWORD

I met Gerard in 1975 when we were students studying at Catholic Junior College. Our paths crossed again when we served our National Service as fellow Army officers and our journey continued when we ended up in Canada pursuing our tertiary education for several years in the early 80s.

After returning to Singapore, we remained close buddies even after getting married and pursuing our respective careers. My family looks forward to the annual Chinese New Year traditional dinner at Gerry's home where we will be treated to a smorgasbord of delicious food, the popular signature dishes are normally those cooked by his mum, aunty Irene.

I have always enjoyed my interactions with Gerry, a very gregarious and fun-loving person. Besides being a foodie himself, Gerry turned out to be quite a good cook as well. He discovered he had this innate talent when circumstances forced him to prepare his own meals during his university days in Canada. He obviously inherited his culinary skills from his mum.

But what makes Gerry so special is that he is very family oriented, family means everything to him. I spent many memorable moments with Gerry's family in his home as well as at the Changi holiday bungalows. The family conversations often revolved around his parents' experiences during the pre-war and colonial days. The highlight of those family gatherings was mealtimes, we will all be salivating just from the aroma of the home cooked dishes emanating from aunty Irene's kitchen.

I have always admired his mother's passion for cooking. She is one of the most generous people I know, and her recipes are a testament to that generosity—they are full of love and care for everyone who tries them.

So, you can imagine what a big honour it was for me when I was approached to write the foreword for this special book.

It's no secret that food is a binding force for families, and it's no surprise that Aunty Irene has been cooking all her life. She started collecting her handwritten notes of thousands of recipes in her countless well-kept notebooks over eight decades!

This book is a treasure trove of flavourful recipes. The 90 specially selected recipes featured in this book is a fitting tribute to aunty Irene's classic culinary delights as she turns 90. Every dish is covered with meticulous detail, including information on its heritage with a clear step by step guide.

Gerry and his mum spent months of relentless research with frequent conversations culminating with this compendium of recipes. It's a legacy to be passed down through generations of the Chai clan and now made available to readers of this book. Food is really a binding force, preserving family recipes and passing them along, honours your lineage.

I hope that anytime you use any of the recipes from this book you are reminded of Aunty Irene's keen sense of curiosity, her willingness to improvise and her deep-rooted passion, qualities which exemplifies her unique brand of cooking.

If you're looking for some inspiration or just wanting something new, then this book is ideal, extremely tasty, it hits all the right notes!

P. Ramakrishna

A LEGACY OF LOVE AND GOOD FOOD

This book is written as a labour of love, a collaboration between mother and son. This is the story of a remarkable woman who has been collecting recipes for over eighty years. It is a celebration of her life, her passion, and her favourite recipes (and there are thousands in her collection) that have been enhanced and perfected through the years. She is a pioneer generation citizen who did her part in educating thousands of children, many of whom became successful doctors, professors, business people, civil servants, entertainers, and so on. This year is her ninetieth birthday, and in this book, she and I share ninety of her favourite recipes, some complex but many simple and some lost through time. The recipes are accompanied by life stories and anecdotes, which serve as a connection to our heritage and a legacy for family and friends. It will hopefully be entertaining as well as relatable for the general reader. Do note that the emphasis is on home-cooked food for home chefs, and the book has thus been presented in that manner.

My mother, Irene, and father, Michael, who passed on some fifteen years ago, tell of a love story and a long-lasting marriage of over fifty years. Pap enjoyed eating; it was his joie de vivre. He insisted on perfection, which Mum was only too happy to provide. She developed a passion for cooking good food from a very young age and is a perfectionist bold enough to persistently ask for a recipe when the dish is tasty. This included pestering family and friends and walking into kitchens and charming the chefs/cooks/waiters for a recipe everywhere around the world as they had travelled widely. Up till today, she carries with her a notebook everywhere she goes to take notes of foods she has enjoyed or to write recipes she's managed to secure. I have lost count of the numerous notebooks and recipe books she possesses, and amazingly, at her age, she is able to find whatever recipe she is looking for – all without the use of technology. Having always lived together, my own family of lovely wife, Diane, and four sons, of course, benefited from Mum's wonderful experiments and sometimes too much of the same thing as she persisted in perfecting a recipe.

Having come from a lineage of Chinese, Peranakan (Baba Chinese), and Parsi and over four generations in Singapore, we share some history and identify members of our family tree whom, I guess, in many ways have shaped our – and certainly my – existence and place within the community at large. You will note that many are just simple ordinary folk whom I believe, all have a story to tell. The recipes we are sharing are not specific in genre but include what Mum and I deem to be delectable recipes, mostly local ones, some lost over time, and some even as simple as comfort food which I enjoyed as a child growing up. You may find some of these recipes in other cookbooks, but Mum's interpretation comes with the painstaking efforts to simplify the process and innovate with 'secret' ingredients and sauces that make them so mouth-wateringly good. I would like to think that this cookbook is different as the recipes are accompanied with stories that are unique and specific to her life and the way in which she obtained them, stories that are perhaps personal to the family, and stories that are in step with the evolution of modern Singapore.

You see, my father was a police officer from the colonial era through modern Singapore who retired a deputy commissioner of police, and my mother was a primary school teacher throughout her career. His career journey from the 1950's through the 1980's was eventful, having been posted to various roles during Singapore's tumultuous years, starting from the police station to reserve unit (riot squad), special branch (Internal Security Department [ISD]), immigration, CID, and eventually Singapore Police Force as deputy commissioner of police. Throughout his career, he was trained and often attended meetings abroad and thus travelled and met colleagues from all over the world, learning and implementing policing strategies that help lay the foundation for today's modern police force. This enabled him to not only meet colleagues globally but also taste the fine culinary offerings of many countries. My mother would often be at his side and chasing after recipes of delicious dishes.

It took some doing for me to persuade Mum to share her recipes. After all, Peranakan women typically carry their recipes to the grave. However, once convinced, Mum, being the perfectionist that she is, insisted on curating and shortlisting the recipes. My hope is that the reader will not only find the recipes delectable but also enjoy reading the stories that accompany them. Our hope is that the home cooks will find these recipes useful and easy enough to prepare such that their families can also enjoy what we have relished over the years. My wife, Diane, who hails from faraway Trinidad and Tobago (I went away to university in Canada and brought back more than what my parents bargained for almost forty years ago) was inspirational and most helpful in the process. She helped with initial editing, plating for the photo shoots, picking family photos and created a mix media painting specially for this book.

For the rest of the family, this book serves as a legacy for you and your children. My advice to you....... learn to cook!

CAST OF CHARACTERS

Mum celebrating her 90th birthday in December 2022

Mum and Pap on their wedding day

Mum and Pap in later years

Pap in uniform

Mama Chit and Kong Kong when they were married

Mama Chit and Kong Kong in later years

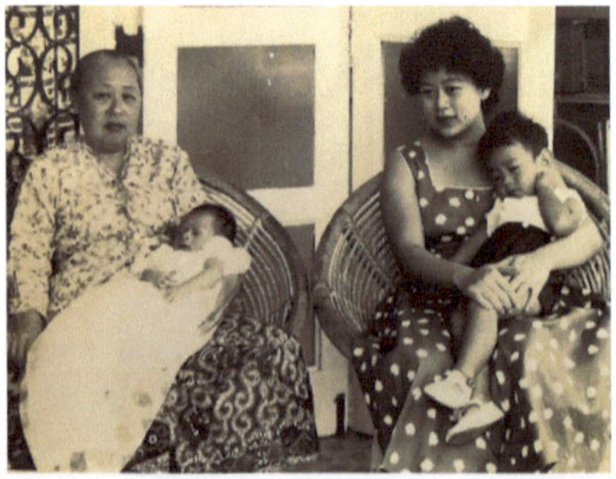

Mama Chit and Mum with her two sons (I'm the one in Mama Chik's arms)

Mum and Pap with their 3 kids at the house in Keng Lee Road

Mama Mary (Pap's mother) in her younger days

Grandpa Joseph (Pap's father) in his early years

Kong Kong's Uncle Muncherjee

Hau Cheh with me and my siblings, Tony and Daphne

Diane, me and our four boys (Christopher, Brendan, Adrian and Dominic) in the late '90's

Mix-media painting by Diane - a collage of photos on a painting
of the old colonial house at Mount Rosie Road

INTRODUCTION

There are literally thousands of cookbooks out there with wonderful recipes and as many that are focused on the Singaporeans' fixation on food. Some include intense research on the history of the dishes and their cultural perspective, many through the lens of a kaleidoscope of the myriad cultures that make Singapore unique, including the fusion of these recipes. When thinking about how to present Mum's favourite recipes, it became a walk-through in time when we started discussing what to include or not. Recognising that older recipes originated at a time when food and ingredients were scarce and perhaps less intriguing, we decided that the older recipes must start from the basics, but these have now been enhanced and perfected over the years using modern ingredients, spices, and sauces that were not available back in the day.

Even though Mum is a perfectionist, she has always tried to simplify the process of cooking as much as possible. The rationale is that if you can get from point A to point B in a straight line, why go through a circuitous route, especially if the outcome is equally brilliant. She was a working mother and brought up three children, and like all busy mothers, there was little time to mess around in the kitchen for hours. Yet as Pap, a self-confessed foodie, possessed a discerning palate, in other words fussy, she had to find ways to shorten the cooking process without taking too many shortcuts. Hence, our target audience of experienced or even less experienced home chefs with a busy schedule may find this useful. One other point to note is that we are sharing recipes and not teaching the audience how to cook. The myriad of cookbooks available in the market and even YouTube do this very well.

Furthermore, I would like to think that this cookbook is different in that the stories accompanying the recipes tell of the life experiences of my parents and in particular my mother and her obsession in wanting to replicate or improve a dish she enjoyed. It also describes how she obtained, evolved, and then perfected the recipes to the very last gram, cup, and teaspoon. This is a story of an ordinary woman talented and passionate about good food, persistent in perfecting dishes suited to local tastes (in particular my father's), and constantly curious about how applying different cooking methods and ingredients affect the outcome of the dish and ultimately its taste. But more than all this, for Mum, it is also pure pleasure to see family and friends enjoy the fruits of her labour in the kitchen. I must add, though, that Mum takes feedback seriously and objectively, and if the feedback was not entirely positive, it would bother her such that she would retrace through every step of the process and ingredients, experiment, and improve on the recipe (regardless of how many times) until she is completely satisfied with the outcome as is the person who provided the feedback. It is almost obsessive in my opinion, but this is the sort of woman that she is.

In the years leading up to modern Singapore, when restaurants and eateries were few and far between and certainly not affordable to the regular person, when there was less hustle and bustle and more time at hand to cook for the family, cooking at home was not just a necessity but also a social activity, particularly for the women and housewives. Friends, neighbours, and family would often visit with a dish in hand; discussions on recipes will ultimately emerge; and the exchange and thereafter testing and improvements of these recipes will follow. This interest and passion for cooking at home, lost for some time, has today been rekindled due to the coronavirus pandemic when the population was forced to stay at home, and restaurants, eateries, and hawker centres were closed or limited in operation. Food delivery has become essential for those who don't enjoy cooking at home, but equally, many home-based food businesses have sprouted, and many more people have found interest in cooking at home again.

This book will hopefully help further rekindle interest in home-cooked food, and by reintroducing recipes that have been lost and forgotten, in sharing some newly concocted ones and some time-tested favourites that have been improved through the years, we hope the reader will enjoy the culinary delights that I have relished all my life. Delivered through a spectrum of time, the recipes have been organised and presented in a chronological journey of Mum's life, beginning from the colonial days through modern Singapore, from pre-war existence through the mundane and sometimes exciting periods of day-to-day working life to marriage and bringing up the family through retirement and afterward and all the life experiences in between.

For less experienced cooks and those who may not be entirely familiar with many of the local terms/ names of dishes and local ingredients, please refer to the glossary for translation and even some history lessons. Do try some of these recipes and bon appétit!

PRE-WAR THROUGH POST-WAR – A TIME WHEN FOOD WAS SCARCE

We kick off this chapter and book with a glimpse of pre-war colonial Singapore circa 1930s. Singapore was then already a well-established free port that specialised in entrepôt trade. However, it was the time of the Great Depression, and Singapore was experiencing a rollercoaster economy much like the rest of the Western world then. Life for the common folk was difficult. Good infrastructure was limited to the business district and southern central parts of the island, and much of the rural areas were still abundant with dense forests and plantations (mostly gambier, rubber, pepper, etc.) along with numerous impoverished kampongs and fishing villages ensconced across the island.

Regardless of the Depression, some local businessmen (mostly Chinese) amassed large fortunes from the trading of rubber, tin, rice, and shipping; and for them and the British colonial masters who governed the country, life was very good. But for the rest of the population, it was really eking out a meagre living. Poverty was rife. It was then that street hawking became even more widespread, particularly for immigrants who saw it as a good way to earn a living. Socially, secret societies were rampant; and apart from collecting 'protection monies' in their territories, they operated gambling dens, illegal immigration, prostitution, extortion, illicit opium dens, and the list goes on. Gang fights were also rampant, and these secret societies were a menace to society.

The description of Singapore by its first prime minister Lee Kuan Yew of those early years was 'I grew up in a Singapore of the 1920s and 1930s. The population was less than a million, and most of Singapore was covered by mangrove swamps, rubber plantations, and secondary forest because rubber had failed, and forests around Mandai/Bukit Timah took its place. In these early decades, the island was riddled with opium houses and prostitution and came to be widely monikered as "Sin-galore".'

Mum grew up in those early years and lived in a rented old bungalow that had wood plank flooring and built on concrete stilts raised above ground. The *dapur* (kitchen), storage room, garage, and outhouse were in a single-storied separate building situated behind the main house. Her father, whom we affectionally addressed as Kong Kong, was a senior clerical staff at the Netherlands Trading Society and had rented the house in the 1920s. He was a generous and benevolent man (probably from his Parsi heritage known to be such) and had willingly taken in relatives from both sides of the family, especially during the war years. During the bombings and after the Japanese landed, he had saved staff and documents at the bank including harbouring the family and many others, hiding them in the bank's premises in Cecil Street. They remained there for a few months, surviving on a large cache of canned foods that had been stocked by the Dutch before the war started.

For his efforts, he received a prestigious medal, the Order of Orange-Nassau from the Dutch monarchy. During World War II, the Order of Orange-Nassau was bestowed upon both members of the Dutch military and members of foreign services who had helped liberate the Netherlands from Nazi occupation and those who helped liberate the former Dutch colonies in the Pacific. It is a chivalric order open to 'everyone who has earned special merits for society'. These are people who deserve appreciation and recognition from society for the special way in which they have carried out their activities. Certainly, he was not one to brag about his activities, but he was quietly very proud of this recognition.

The family returned home when the situation settled, and the Japanese occupation government was in place. Thus began a living routine that was highly restricted with limited food and resources and the lingering fear of Japanese soldiers and the feared *Kempeitai* (military police arm of the Imperial Japanese Army), who would occasionally come by the house to check on 'nefarious' activity. It was then that Mum, her sisters, and her cousins would hide under the house. On one occasion, their only brother, who possessed a home-made crystal radio, was caught and taken away. He was beaten and tortured and finally when he returned was afflicted with a stammer for the rest of his life.

Besides Kong Kong's family of six children and the relatives he sheltered, there would be no less than twenty people staying in the house at any time during the occupation years. Never a dull moment, I was told, but what a tremendous challenge to feed all when food was scarce. Kong Kong would somehow find the food, and Mum's mother, whom we affectionately called Mama Chit, would somehow multiply what little there was to feed everyone. As much as possible, everyone chipped in and did their part to supplement the food store. During the three and a half years of Japanese occupation, there was hardly any schooling, so Mum, who was then 11 years old, also worked. She was able to pick up Japanese easily and was quite fluent in conversation, so she was hired to man the telephone in a home factory. She was paid all of $200 (the Japanese-issued dollar then popularly known as 'banana money') and sixteen *katis* of rice a month. Occasionally, she would receive a slab of pork, which was much appreciated by the family.

Their house was located along Keng Lee Road facing the Bukit Timah Canal, not too far from Norfolk Road, where Lee Kuan Yew lived. As a child during the early war years, Mum would be playing with cousins and friends in the drain fronting the house alongside the road when Lee Kuan Yew, then in his early twenties, would ride his bicycle along Keng Lee Road on his way home in the evening. They would very cheekily pelt him with stones as he rode by calling out, 'Oh, Harry!' He would very nonchalantly look back and proceed to ignore them. Little did they know then that he would eventually rise to be the father of modern Singapore.

In those early 1960s years, my memories of the house at Keng Lee Road were always filled with fun and food. We would run around, playing hide-and-seek with my cousins whenever we visited. I swear the house was haunted as I saw on several occasions a white figure squatting on top of the outhouse or sometimes the kitchen. That scared the living daylights out of us – very quickly, we'd troop back into the house and no more hide-and-seek until the next visit. Unfortunately, the house was destroyed in the floods of 1969, and today an apartment building stands in its place.

1. Babi Pangang Jam (Roasted Pork Belly Jam)

Mum acquired this recipe when she was just 7 years old. (Yes, her interest goes that far back!) Growing up in Keng Lee Road, she had childhood friends living in a Hainanese community house accommodating several families in a lane behind the house, what is today Suffolk Road. Many of the families eked out a living as street hawkers, peddling food around the Farrer Park or Newton areas. Approaching an uncle one day who specialised in roasted belly pork, she asked him for the recipe and how to prepare it. His reply was, 'Little girl, why do you want to know? You are too young to be interested in this.'

Her reply was, 'Uncle, I will grow up one day, and I want to make this.' That was a good enough response – he gave her the recipe.

In this segment, we are not sharing the roasted belly pork recipe; you can find this in many recipe books or even buy good, finished products at Cold Storage, NTUC FairPrice, other supermarkets, food courts, or hawker centres. What is special here is the jam (that's what Mum calls it) or the marinade that was used for basting and thereafter as a spread over the roasted pork when it was being served, much like the dish that was served at the now closed Yet Con Restaurant in Purvis Street. This style is almost impossible to find in the market today. We also share a chili sauce recipe to accompany the dish that enhances the overall flavour of roasted belly pork.

Main Ingredients

10 shallots
2 slices of lengkuas *(blue ginger)*
2 tsp five-spice powder
1 tbsp ketumbar *(coriander) powder*
1 tsp salt
3 tsp sugar

Additional Ingredients

2 tsp dark soya sauce
1 tsp light soya sauce
1 tsp sweet black sauce

Method

- Grind the main ingredients into a fine paste.
- Fry ground ingredients with 4 tbsp of oil till fragrant and add sauces.
- Spread the jam over roasted pork.

Note: For the chilli sauce, use 4 tbsp of Koon Yick Wah Kee chilli sauce (sailboat brand) and 2 tbsp of sweet sauce, diluting with a little hot water.

2. *Babi Tausi* (Pork in Black Beans)

At the onset of the war, Mum was 10 years old. Food was scarce, but even then, as difficult and as meagre as food supplies were, there were still tasty dishes. Her mother, Mama Chit, although uneducated, was always resourceful enough to scrounge and feed her family and an extended family of twenty. One dish in particular, *babi tausi*, that Mum remembers well and still cooks today comes with a story she never fails to relate whenever serving this dish.

In the early days of the war, when air raids were still rife, the family constructed their own bomb shelter at home – a large hardwood dining table covered with mattresses on top and on every side. The children and even adults (as many as it would fit) would cram under the table when the sirens went off. It was a terrifying time for a child, but she remembers how famished they would be after the raids. A vivid memory of a large pot of *babi tausi* would be on a nearby table, and in those days, any cut of pork would be a bonus. A plate of rice or sometimes a gruel of rice mixed with tapioca and a scoop of *babi tausi* would taste heavenly. Naturally, vinegar was used in the dish to preserve it for much longer as there was no refrigeration then. Today, of course, the recipe suggests a more specific cut of pork, primarily trotters. When accompanied with *sambal belachan* or even chicken rice chilli sauce, the result is no less heavenly!

Ingredients

2 pork trotters (front legs recommended)
1 tbsp tausi *(black beans)*
2 tbsp taucheo *paste*
1 tbsp garlic paste
1 tbsp sugar
1 tbsp vinegar
350 ml water

Method

- Blanch the trotters. Place in room temperature water and bring to a boil to cleanse the meat. Remove from water and dry when done.
- Marinate the pork with black beans, *taucheo*, and garlic paste.
- Fry the pork and add the sugar and vinegar.
- Add in the water and bring to a boil, then simmer for an hour till tender. (Alternatively, place in a Crockpot and let it simmer for two hours.)

Note: If preferred, you can use pork belly.

3. Nyonya Laksa *Lemak*

Most know that laksa originates from the Peranakan culture, a combination of local spices in a rich and spicy coconut-flavoured soup and Chinese noodles. The fascinating thing about this recipe is that Mum had discovered a more delectable variant, one even better than her mother's recipe, once again from the same Hainanese community house in Suffolk Road. Pestering another uncle who was a laksa street hawker, he finally gave in to a very pesky 12-year-old. What is amusing about this story is that a Nyonya would believe that a laksa dish from a Hainanese hawker is even better than traditional Peranakan recipes – outrageous. Interestingly, though, it is the same basic recipe that she uses to this very day, albeit with some modifications to the overall presentation. She now also adds new ingredients that enhances the overall flavour of the dish that was not available back then, for example, salted egg yolk paste.

Serves between five and six people

Main Ingredients

30 g lengkuas *(blue ginger)*
100 g shallots
1 fresh red chilli
2 cm turmeric
2 tsp chilli paste
1 clove of garlic
1½ stalks of serai *(lemongrass)*
3 candlenuts (soaked in hot water)
½ tbsp ketumbar *(coriander) powder*
20 g belachan
¼ cube fish seasoning
¼ cube chicken seasoning
¼ tbsp sugar
½ tsp salt
¼ tbsp salted egg yolk paste

Additional Ingredients

45 g dried prawns (soaked in 120 ml hot water, saving the residual broth)
Prawn shells, boiled to obtain 120 ml prawn stock
250 g coconut cream (equivalent to first squeeze or pati santan*)*
125 g coconut milk (equivalent to second squeeze) mixed with 25 ml evaporated milk and 650 ml water
850 g laksa bee hoon *(available in markets), scalded*
750 gm taugeh *(bean sprouts), scalded*

Garnish

500 g de-shelled fresh prawns, boiled quickly till red
2 fish cakes, grilled and shredded
1½ cucumber, shredded
10 g daun kesum *(Vietnamese coriander or laksa leaves), shredded*
sambal for laksa (see 'Basic Rempah *and Sauces')*

Method for Gravy

- Grind main ingredients into a fine paste.
- Fry ground ingredients with 3 tbsp of oil till fragrant and *pechah minyak* (oil breaking or oil splitting from the *rempah*).
- Add the mixture of dried prawn broth, prawn stock, and coconut milk.
- Bring to a boil, then add the dried prawns.
- Finally, add the coconut cream.
- Further, salt and sugar may be added according to taste.

Finishing

- When serving, place the scalded noodles and bean sprouts into a bowl, add slices of de-shelled prawn and fish cake on the noodles, and pour boiling gravy generously over the noodles.
- Garnish with shredded cucumber, laksa leaves, and laksa sambal. (see Basic Rempah and Sauces)

4. Curry *Yahudi* (Jewish Curry)

An older Jewish lady who lived in Mount Sophia Road gave this recipe to Mama Chit in the 1930s. They were *cherki kakis* – a group of lady friends who played the Peranakan card game *cherki* and often would chew *sireh* (betel nut), gossip, and share recipes in the process. She had lived in Singapore (or the region) for many years, seeing the southern Indian culinary influence in the dish. What we find different about this chicken curry is the inclusion of dates, which is not typical in most curries but certainly adds a sweetness to the dish.

Ingredients A

5 shallots
5 cloves of garlic

Ingredients B

1 tsp turmeric powder
100 g shallots
1½ tsp chilli powder
½ tsp clove powder
1 tbsp ketumbar *(coriander) powder*
¼ tsp white pepper
1 tsp cumin powder
1 tsp fennel powder

Ingredients C

600 g chicken
1 large onion, sliced
180 ml coconut cream
10 dates, sliced lengthwise into four then halved, soaked in boiling water just enough to cover the dates

Method

- Grind ingredients A into a fine paste for marinade.
- Marinate the chicken with ingredients A for 2 hours.
- Mix ingredients B with ¼ cup of water to form a paste.
- Fry the big onion, then add in the paste.
- Add the chicken to the paste, then add the coconut cream.
- When the meat is almost cooked, add in the dates including the water.
- Bring to a boil and add a pinch of salt and sugar to taste.
- Serve when ready.

5. Parsi Bread Pudding

As mentioned in the foreword, there is Parsi heritage in my family. This comes from Mum's side, whose great-grandfather was a Parsi gentleman from Bombay. He settled in Singapore and married a Peranakan woman. (It was rumoured that they eloped, and he whisked her away on a white horse. Right!) The gentleman was known as Rustamji Palonji-Mehta, who adapted more to the local Baba Chinese culture as Parsis in Singapore were few and far between in those days. Seems this is still the case today. They had six children, and only one was married, from which Mum's lineage is traced. This old bread pudding recipe uses ingredients that are different from your everyday bread pudding. It includes macaroni and has a rich and firm texture to it. Enjoy!

Ingredients

1 large French loaf (about 350 g in weight)
¾ tin of Carnation evaporated milk
1 tin of water (measure by Carnation tin)
300 g sugar
180 g boiled macaroni
3½ egg whites (save the yolks)
2 tsp allspice powder
180 g butter
120 g sliced almonds (toasted)
50 g sultanas
50 g candied orange peel

Method

- Slice the French loaf, toast, and then butter the toasted slices.
- Boil the evaporated milk, water, allspice powder, and sugar.
- Soak the buttered toasts into the solution and mash with a fork.
- Mix in the sultanas, macaroni, and sliced almonds.
- Whisk the egg whites and fold evenly into the mixture.
- Bake in the oven at 200°C for one hour.
- Stir yolk with some butter.
- Midway through baking, glaze the bread pudding with the yolk mixture.
- Continue baking and finish again with the remainder of the glaze and bake till dry.

6. Old-Fashioned Butter Cake

This was Mama Chit's favourite butter cake recipe. Using basic implements, she would churn out numerous cakes at a time, often baking in biscuit tins without the convenience of an electric cake mixer or modern oven. Butter cake was mandatory for her household, especially during Chinese New Year festivities back in the day. Today there are tons of butter cake recipes out there, but this simple one with all the ingredients and proportions laid out does result in a fine and rich butter cake. Of course, you can now use modern appliances to help lighten the workload and shorten the preparation time.

Ingredients

2 blocks of butter, softened
300 g sugar
400 g cake flour
2 tsp baking powder
12 eggs
3 tbsp evaporated milk
2 tsp brandy
3 tsp vanilla essence

Method

- Cream the butter and sugar till white.
- Beat the eggs till light and add to the butter mixture.
- Sift the flour and baking powder and fold lightly into the butter mixture.
- Add the evaporated milk, brandy, and vanilla essence into the mixture.
- Bake in a 25 × 25 × 5 cm greased cake pan at 180°C for 45–60 minutes.

Note: Should you want a marble effect, then remove 3 tbsp of batter into a bowl and add 1 tbsp of cocoa powder and a touch of milk. Stir the mixed cocoa batter into the plain batter to create the marble effect. Butter cake being so flexible, then nuts such as almonds and walnut can be added if variety is desired.

7. Tapioca Sponge Cake

This is a recipe from Mum's elder sister Auntie Amy, who was able to make a lovely sponge cake even with the limited ingredients available during the Japanese occupation. The only thing available in abundance was tapioca, often home-grown or plentiful in public wooded areas or in the jungle. Flour and butter were limited in supply, expensive, and difficult to acquire. Also, the oven used was old-fashioned cast iron and charcoal fired. Hence, Auntie Amy was immensely popular with her younger siblings and family, especially during birthdays, as she was still able to make a fluffy sponge cake. The recipe uses tapioca and requires grating, hence a little more tedious to prepare today unless, of course, you have an electric grater. However, we share this recipe not only because it is authentic and good but also because it does provide a glimpse into a time when you could not take anything for granted, and you use whatever is available. Necessity is the mother of invention.

Ingredients

1 kg tapioca
200 g sugar
4 eggs
1 coconut squeezed for first milk or 1 box (200 g) coconut cream
1 tsp salt

Method

- Grate the tapioca, wash it, then squeeze dry.
- Spread the grated tapioca and air in the sun for 1–2 hours.
- Cook the coconut cream with a pinch of salt and bring to a boil.
- When the coconut cream is cool, mix in the beaten eggs and the dry, grated tapioca.
- Bake in a greased cake pan at 200°C for 1 hour.

8. Nasi *Lemak Kukus* (Steamed Coconut-Flavoured Rice)

Nasi *lemak* is the rich, aromatic rice dish derived from the use of coconut milk and pandan leaves. To the Peranakans, how the rice is prepared is important; and in the early years, serving nasi *lemak* accompanied by numerous dishes was considered a grand dining affair. Often served at weddings and important family events, Mum learnt this recipe in the 1940s from her mother's elder sister Thwa Yi, a diminutive figure who stood all of four feet six inches. She bore seventeen children! The family lived in a house with a large compound on Kampong Java Road. Mum remembers it vividly as a child attending weddings, and I suppose there were many, given the numerous children Thwa Yi had. The weddings were held in the garden, furnished with many rented tables, and Mum and her cousins would be running around and playing in between tables. She remembers the large *kuali* (wok) that Thwa Yi used for cooking over a large coal fire and imagined then that it was big enough to have a bath in or for use as a boat during floods, which were common in those days. It was a child's imagination then, but what is real today is the fluffy, fragrant, and flavourful nasi *lemak kukus* recipe that we share. *Kukus* means steamed, which makes a world of difference to the nasi *lemak* as compared with the customary boiling method. Many of the recipes for the accompanying dishes are also shared in various sections of the book with notations.

Ingredients

600 g superior-quality Thai rice mixed with 30 g glutinous rice (serves 6–7 people)
250 g first milk of 1 fresh or equivalent of 250 g coconut cream
4 pandan leaves
1½ tsp salt
¼ tbsp sugar
360 g water

Method

- Soak the rice for 3–4 hours.
- Drain the rice and steam in a perforated steamer together with 2 pandan leaves for 10 minutes only. (The rice must be grainy but not cooked.)
- Transfer the rice into a basin and soak it with 250 g coconut cream and 360 g water.
- Add salt and sugar and soak for a few hours until the rice has absorbed all the liquid.
- Place the rice back in the steamer with 2 new pandan leaves and steam for another 20 minutes.
- The rice will be cooked shiny and grainy.

Note: Dishes that we typically serve with nasi *lemak kukus* include sambal *belachan*, Peranakan satay *babi*, *udang goreng assam*, Peranakan sambal *timun*, egg sambal *tumis*, sambal *ikan bilis*, *otak otak*, sambal *kangkong*, and *assam ikan tamban*.

9. Mama's Roast

This is another recipe that dates to the pre-war colonial era. This was Mama Chit's attempt at a Western-styled dish in an old Peranakan kitchen. I am sure the Western flavour of this dish comes from using Worchester (Lea & Perrins) sauce and A1 Steak Sauce 😉, which have been around since the 1800s. Of course, the inclusion of local soya sauce adds to the local flavours in the dish; but in all honesty, it is tasty. Mum calls the dish Mama's roast, but it is, in fact, fried, then cooked. In the original recipe, the outcome is like a roast chicken with little or no gravy. It could be more like a stew if you add water and thicken the sauce, which in fact is a comfort food for my sons, especially when served with French loaf or mashed potatoes.

Ingredients

1 chicken (about 900 g)
½ tsp salt
1 tbsp Lea & Perrins sauce
1½ tsp of A1 sauce
1 tbsp of light soya sauce
3 tbsp of flour
½ tsp chicken seasoning powder
½ tsp dark soya sauce
½ tbsp garlic paste

Additional Ingredients

2 tbsp butter
½ tsp sugar

Method

- Cut the chicken into bite sizes.
- Marinate the chicken with the combined ingredients.
- Fry the chicken with butter, adding ½ tsp sugar.
- Add a little water and cook till gravy is thick.

Note: The original recipe comes with a little thick gravy. Add more water if a stew-like consistency is preferred.

10. Ayam Goreng Manis (Sweet Fried Chicken)

During the early years before the war, Mama Chit employed a young helper, a Boyanese girl, who helped around the kitchen and performed other household duties. She learnt to cook from Mama Chit, and very quickly, not only did she become competent, but she started to enjoy cooking as well. She shared this old Boyan recipe. The Boyanese come from the island of Pulau Bawean, located off the northern coast of Java, Indonesia, more than 1,200 km south of Singapore. I am quite sure travel time in those days must have been horrendous and difficult as it still is even today. Many Boyanese still work and live in Singapore. This recipe uses a multitude of spices and ingredients, and when cooked, the chicken is tender, flavourful, and tantalising when combined with *rempah* (spice paste). Served with white rice, this was one of Kong Kong's favourite dishes.

Ingredients A

1 tbsp chilli paste
8 shallots
6 chilli padi *(optional)*
1 cm turmeric
2 cloves of garlic
4 slices galangal (blue ginger)
2 stalks of lemongrass
20 g belachan
2 cm ginger

Ingredients B

2 tbsp coriander powder
1 tsp fennel powder
1 tsp cumin powder

Ingredients C

1 big onion, sliced
2 kaffir lime leaves, sliced
1 turmeric leaf, sliced

Ingredients D

2½ cm cinnamon bark
6 cloves
6 cardamoms
1 cm nutmeg

Additional Ingredients

1 whole chicken or equivalent in parts (800 g)
180 ml coconut milk
1 tbsp kerisik *paste (dry shredded coconut paste)*
1 tbsp tamarind juice, mixed with some water to form a watery paste
2 tsp sugar

Method

- o Grind ingredients A into a fine paste.
- o Mixed ingredients B with some water to form a paste.
- o Marinate the chicken with ingredients A and B for 1 hour.
- o Fry ingredients C with 3 tbsp of oil, then add ingredients D.
- o Add in the marinated chicken and slowly fry till fragrant.
- o Add 180 ml coconut milk, then cook till chicken is almost tender.
- o Finally, add in the tamarind juice, *kerisik*, and sugar.
- o Serve with white rice.

11. Dalcha (Lentil Stew)

Kong Kong was a quarter Parsi whose grandfather had supposedly whisked off his bride on a white horse. Kong Kong's father was one of six children from the marriage and was the only child who got married—to a Cantonese woman. They had four children, and unfortunately, Kong Kong's father passed away when he was just 4 years old. (He was the eldest, so his folks must have had one child every year.) He did keep up with his Parsi cultural heritage from his aunts and uncles, especially with his uncle Muncherjee, as the family moved in with him when Kong Kong's father passed away. This recipe came from one of Kong Kong's aunts and interestingly uses coconut milk, which is more akin to the southern Indian style. I guess he preferred it that way, and it was comfort food for him, dating back to the early 1900s. He would have Mama Chit prepare this dish for him almost weekly – he was just comfortable with it and enjoyed eating this lentil stew with rice.

Ingredients

1 cup or 128 g dahl *(red lentils)*
700 ml water
¼ cup coconut milk
¼ tsp clove powder
¼ tsp cinnamon powder
½ tsp fennel powder
2 cloves of garlic, ground
1 cm turmeric, ground
2 tsp cardamom powder

Additional Ingredients

4 boiled eggs
fried shallots

Method

- Rinse the *dahl* and soak for at least an hour. Soaking longer will make the *dahl* creamier.
- Boil the *dahl* in three cups of water till thick. (Some may prefer to mash the *dahl.*)
- Add in the coconut milk.
- Add the garlic and turmeric paste.
- Add in the clove, cinnamon, fennel, and cardamom powder and keep boiling.
- Add four boiled eggs.
- Add salt to taste and garnish with fried shallots and a pinch of pepper.

12. Rendang Padang

Rendang is an immensely popular Minang dish originating from the Minangkabau region of Padang in West Sumatra, Indonesia. It has spread across Indonesian cuisine to the those of neighbouring Southeast Asian countries. This Rendang Padang recipe is another old one that came from a small pondok-style eatery along Jalan Pinang in the Arab Street district. Mama Chit frequented the eatery when they were still operating in the late 1930s. She loved the beef rendang served there. Befriending the Indonesian lady cook, she finally managed to get the recipe. Hmmm, I guess obtaining recipes runs in the family. The beef rendang when stewed till tender is succulent and flavourful, and the *rempah* is delicious and aromatic. Rendang goes well with various rice dishes like nasi *lemak* or even with *lontong*. Alternatively, the same recipe can apply to chicken or mutton, if preferred.

Ingredients A

10 shallots
5 cloves of garlic
1 cm turmeric
1½ cm ginger
1½ cm blue ginger
2 candlenuts
2 tbsp dry chilli paste
1 tbsp taucheo *(brown) paste*
20 gm belachan
2 tbsp ketumbar *(coriander) powder*
1 tsp jeera (roasted cumin seeds) powder
1 tsp jintan manis *(fennel seeds) powder*

Ingredients B

2 stalks of lemongrass, bruised
3 daun salam *(local bay leaf)*
2 daun limau perut *(kaffir lime leaves)*
2 petals of bunga kantan *(torch ginger flower)*

Ingredients C

1 kg beef (preferably beef knuckle cut into large chunks)
250 ml coconut milk
1 tbsp tamarind mixed with some water to form a 60 ml watery paste
1 tbsp kerisik *paste (dry shredded coconut paste)*
1 tbsp sugar
1 chicken seasoning cube

Method

- Grind ingredients A into a fine paste.
- Use 1 tbsp of the paste to marinate the beef.
- Pressure-cook the beef for 16 minutes.
- Fry ingredients A till fragrant and oil breaks, then add the beef. Stir and coat well.
- Add ingredients B, then coconut milk, tamarind paste, and chicken cube.
- Cook till the meat is tender and *rempah* is nice and thick, then add in the *kerisik*.
- Remove the lemongrass stalks and leaves and serve.

13. Loh Kai Yik (Braised Chicken Wings)

This is an old and traditional dish sold by wandering street hawkers as far back as the 1940s and 1950s. This hawker would go by my grandparents' Keng Lee Road home on a tricycle with a platform in the front on which sat a continuously simmering large vat that contained the *loh kai yik* and the hawker himself. The hawker was a large, obese man who served the food, and a much fitter assistant would be pedalling the tricycle. Traditional *loh kai yik* is a stewed dish that included chicken wings, pig skin, pork offal, alkaline cuttlefish, *tau pok* (tofu puffs), and *kangkong* (water spinach) in a flavourful thick gravy. This was so popular with the family that they bought it at least two or three times a week. Mum became friendly with the hawker and occasionally gave him and his assistant a cup of coffee to take a break whenever they came by. On one of these occasions, she popped the question, and he obliged with the recipe. Mum has adapted this recipe to suit more discerning and healthy-eating palettes and hence leaves the offal out but has included belly pork in its place. It goes well with a steaming bowl of white rice.

Ingredients

500 g chicken wings
500 g belly pork, cut into strips
300 g pork skin, washed, scalded, and cut into 10ccm squares
2 large alkaline sotong (squid), cut into 5.0 × 2.5 cm pieces
20 brown tau pok *(tofu puffs), scalded, drained, and squeezed*
600 g kangkong, *(water spinach) – washed, scalded, and knot in small bunches*
8 slices ginger
3 tbsp garlic paste
6 pieces lam yee *(preserved bean curd)*
4 tbsp brown taucheo *paste*
4 tbsp sugar
2 tbsp ginger juice
½ tbsp salt
2 tbsp light soya sauce
6 tbsp red hoisin sauce
1 tbsp chicken seasoning powder

Method

- Heat 6 tbsp of oil and fry the ginger, garlic, *lam yee*, and *taucheo*, then the remainder of the ingredients.
- Add in the pork, pork skin, chicken wings, and 250 ml water and cook for 20 minutes.
- Remove the chicken wings so that it is not overcooked and continue cooking, adding another 250 ml water.
- When pork is almost tender, add in the chicken wings, *kangkong*, *tau pok*, and sotong.
- The gravy should be thick and is ready to serve with rice and chicken rice chilli sauce.

14. Peranakan Nasi *Ulam* (Peranakan Rice Salad)

Here is another of Mama Chit's old recipes. Nasi *ulam* in Malay translates into 'rice salad' and uses numerous local raw herbs and vegetables as the main ingredients, all mixed into the rice. There is a wide variation of nasi *ulam* across Southeast Asia, but the Peranakan version uses herbs and spices that are typical of Peranakan flavours representing the combination of Chinese and Malay cultures in the dish. It can be quite complex in its production; however, Mama Chit's recipe is simpler in form but no less delicious. And as always, sambal *belachan* is a mandatory accompaniment to the dish.

Ingredients A

6 candlenuts
6 shallots
60 gm of belachan

Ingredients B

2 limau purut *(kaffir lime) leaves*
4 petals bunga kantan *(torch ginger)*
4 turmeric leaves
½ cup mint leaves
6 long beans, diced
½ cup basil leaves
1 cucumber, diced with skin on
¼ cup daun kesum *(laksa leaves)*
¼ cup cilantro

Ingredients C

3 bowls of cold cooked rice
500 g ikan tenggiri *(mackerel), grilled, deboned, and broken into small pieces*
600 g medium-sized prawns, marinated with 1 tsp sugar, boiled in 150 ml water, de-shelled, and diced (save the prawn stock)
¼ cup garlic
¼ cup shallots
¼ cup dried prawns, washed and pounded

Method

- Grind ingredients A into a fine paste.
- Fry ingredients A in 2 tbsp of oil till nice and slightly crisp, then add 120 ml prawn stock and cook till thickened.
- Fry the chopped garlic, shallots, and dried prawns.
- Mix the prawns, *tenggiri*, fried Ingredients A, and ingredients B into the rice.
- Finally, mix in the fried garlic, shallots, and dried prawns.
- Dish is ready to serve with sambal *belachan* on the side.

MARRIAGE AND RAISING A FAMILY

When my parents married, Mum was a schoolteacher at Waterloo Girl's School, and Pap was a young police inspector. They had what you might call a classic middle-class wedding – nuptial vows at St Joseph's Church in the morning, followed by lunch at the iconic Cathay Restaurant, then dinner at the then extremely popular Wing Choon Yuen (now Spring Court) Restaurant at Great World.

Having already described Mum's Peranakan-Parsi heritage, Pap's was equally interesting. On his maternal side of the family, his mother, Mary or Mama as we called her, was a second-generation Singaporean of Cantonese descent. Her mother was wealthy, an opium smoker constantly accompanied by a *mui tsai* ('little sister' in Cantonese, describing young Chinese women who worked as domestic servants in affluent Chinese households in traditional Chinese society).

Mama was quite an amazing woman. Educated and a registered nurse, this was unusual and quite an achievement at the time for a local woman. She pursued her nursing career till the late 1960s and rose to the rank of Sister. Posted to a British hospital in Kuching, Sarawak, in the late 1920s, she met her future husband, Joseph, a Hakka-Bidayuh male nurse at the same hospital.

He descended from the mass arrival of Hakkas from China to Sarawak/Borneo during the gold rush in the middle of the eighteenth century and a product of intermarriage with the Bidayuh tribal people. How they came to eventually settle in Singapore is an amusing story. Joseph was a sizeable man with a fondness for alcohol. Having gotten quite inebriated one night, he went to the hospital in search of his girlfriend Mama, who was working the night shift, to borrow money so that he could continue drinking. Causing a ruckus, a male attendant who was trying to quieten him received a punch in his face for his efforts that floored him. Fearing that he would get into trouble, Grandpa Joseph quickly decided that his future lay in Singapore! Having left his hometown and relatives and not knowing anyone in Singapore except Mama, he eventually left behind his Hakka heritage and, like Mum's great-grandfather, adopted his intended spouse's culture, which was in this case Cantonese.

Mama was a stoic woman and the matriarch of the family. Being a working mother in a job that often entailed long hours and later with three children in tow, Mama needed help, so she employed a *ma cheh* to help raise her children (discussed in the next chapter). She was the main breadwinner and struggled to raise the family as, unfortunately, Joseph was not as productive in his career and had passed away when her children were young. Hence, I never had the opportunity to meet him and do not really know much about him. Sadly and for whatever strange reason, none of the older folk spoke much about him.

Mum and Pap married in 1956 and eventually also had three children. Like all young parents, they were working hard through the stormy years – 1957 through 1961 – when the children were born. It was during these tough times when civil servants had to take pay cuts that Pap even went with a crew cut to save money at the barbers. This was a time when Singapore was finding its feet after gaining independence from the British, and newly configured political parties were battling to form a government. All through this, Mum, who had married into a Cantonese family, continued to collect and experiment with recipes.

I suppose her 'value added' in those early years was bringing Peranakan cooking into the home, which of course my father enjoyed. However, not as easily accepted by a traditional Cantonese family with a live-in *ma cheh*, it took a while before Peranakan dishes eventually became part of the household cuisine. You see, Peranakans are descendants of early Chinese migrants who settled in Penang, Malacca, Singapore, and Indonesia, intermarrying with local indigenous peoples. The Peranakan cuisine is therefore a fusion of Chinese, Malay, Javanese, south Indian, and other influences, in contrast to the milder Cantonese cuisine. Mama made the effort and ensured that there was always crispy pork lard in the kitchen, thinking that it was standard fare in Peranakan dishes—not always.

Of course, most of the Peranakan recipes came from Mum's mother, Mama Chit, whom she had learnt a lot from, but interestingly, she was never encouraged to do so. Mama Chit wanted better for her daughters, always reminding them that it was not good to be a slave to the kitchen, like she was. You see, Mama Chit, like her sister Thwa Yi, was a small woman (four feet nine inches tall) and uneducated but possessed a talent for cooking, great wisdom, and a big heart. She was a real Peranakan woman who only conversed in Baba Malay.

Up until her passing in the late 1970s, she would go out occasionally to socialise, gossip, and chit-chat over a *cherki* card game (a popular card game originating from Malacca played by the Nyonyas of olden days) with her fellow Nyonya *kakis* (buddies). Mama Chit would be all dressed up in a sarong kebaya with a handkerchief draped over one shoulder and armed with a *sirih* box filled with betel nut leaves, *pinang*, gambier, *kapor*, and tobacco. Chewing the content was an important social and cultural function back in the day but would leave the user with black-stained teeth and red-stained lips, which is one of the things I fondly remember of her. I reckon she was addicted to the buzz that came along with chewing the stuff.

Coming back to Mama Chit's lack of enthusiasm to teach her daughters how to cook, fortunately, Mum was persistent; she had a good career as a primary school teacher but never lost interest in cooking – thank goodness. So in this section, we share some Peranakan recipes all from Mama Chit's kitchen that date back to those tumultuous years. You will notice that the dishes are all titled in Malay or Peranakan patois. I will attempt my best to translate these to English. We also include a couple of other recipes that Mum picked up along the way in her early married life. Of course, all these dishes have evolved through the years, but the basics remain.

1. Gerang Assam Ikan (Spicy and Sour Fish Stew)

For this dish, Mum recommends fresh Spanish mackerel or threadfin. Mama Chit's version was different from other recipes, typical of Peranakan cuisine; each home did and still does their cooking slightly differently. This is a soupy version that not only uses *assam* (tamarind) but when combined with spices and *kiam chye* (salted mustard greens) also imparts a sourish, salty kick to the dish. Flavourful and fragrant, when served with white rice, it is tasty and extraordinarily satisfying.

Ingredients A

2 bruised stalks of serai *(lemongrass)*
5 slices of lengkuas *(blue ginger)*
1.5 cm piece of kunyit *(turmeric)*
6 buah keras *(candlenut)*
50 g belachan
3 fresh red chillies or ½ tbsp chilli paste
8 shallots

Ingredients B

450 g fish, preferably Spanish mackerel or threadfin
¼ tsp salt
½ tbsp assam *(tamarind)*
1 tomato
½ cup salted mustard greens

Method

- Grind ingredients A into a fine paste. Fry the paste in 2–3 tbsp of oil until it is well cooked (or until *pechah minyak*, translated as oil breaking or oil splitting from the *rempah*).
- Add a pinch of salt.
- Mix ½ tbsp of tamarind with 1 cup of water and add into the fried ingredients.
- Add in 1 tomato sliced in half and ½ cup of salted mustard greens that have been thoroughly washed to lessen its saltiness.
- Add in the fish and boil till cooked. If the preference is for a larger amount of soup, add water according to need.
- When ready and to enhance the taste, add a little sugar.

2. Sambal Belachan (Spicy *Belachan* Relish)

I thought I should cover this particularly important condiment early as sambal *belachan* is a basis for Peranakan cooking and used as an accompanying side sauce to many dishes. *Belachan* is a shrimp paste primarily made from finely crushed shrimp or krill mixed with salt and then fermented for weeks. Made of fermented shrimp, you would expect it to have a pungent odour. (It does and can really be quite offensive to the unaccustomed.) The sambal (relish) using *belachan*, red chillies, and sugar can be refrigerated and later used for preparing dishes or as a side sauce. In fact, this side sauce is usually on the table of every Peranakan meal, including nasi *lemak*, and is most certainly a staple. It is simple to produce but so important to Peranakan cuisine. Here is Mum's Peranakan sambal *belachan* recipe.

Ingredients

8 fresh red chillies
2 tsp sugar
85 g belachan *(toasted), typically half the weight of the chillies*

Method

- Toast the *belachan* until slightly brown. Remove and allow it to cool.
- Grind all the ingredients but not too finely, and the result is sambal *belachan*.
- If preferred, calamansi juice may be added when serving.
- The sambal may be frozen and later thawed when required.

3. Udang/Ikan Masak Nanas (Pineapple Prawn/Fish Soup)

Fresh prawns or Pomfret cooked with spices and sweet pineapple lend to an aromatic and flavourful soupy dish. When ready and to enhance the flavour and spiciness of the dish, add sambal *belachan* and a touch of oil. The Malaccan Peranakans add coconut milk to thicken the soup.

Ingredients A -

200 g shallots
60 g lengkuas *(blue ginger)*
2.5 cm piece of kunyit *(turmeric)*
6 buah keras *(candlenuts)*
50 g belachan
40 g dried red chillies

Ingredients B

500 g large prawns or a 600 g pomfret, depending on preference
300 g sweet pineapple, sliced
¼ tsp salt
½ tsp sugar
1 tsp sambal belachan
30 g assam *(tamarind flesh) mixed with 80 ml water*
4 cups water (~1 litre)
2 tsp oil
1 tsp calamansi juice

Method

- Grind ingredients A into a fine paste.
- Boil the ground ingredients and pineapple in four cups of water.
- Add the prawns, assam juice, sugar, and salt and boil till cooked.
- When cooked, blend the *belachan*, oil, and calamansi juice into a mixture and add into the prawn soup.

4. Nangka Masak Lemak (Jackfruit Cooked in Coconut Cream)

This dish uses young jackfruit that when cooked in coconut milk balances its earthy flavour. Often used as a meat substitute for vegans, young jackfruit has a fibre-like consistency. When it is ripe, it produces a strong fruity odour and a sweet flavour. Many confuse it with durian, but they are quite different and are, in fact, distinct species, even though they look alike. Hence, it is best to use the unripe young version, which soaks in the flavour of the spices and coconut cream. Popular in Peranakan and Malay households, this version dates back to Mum's growing up years.

Ingredients A

4 cloves of garlic
1 tbsp dried chilli paste
6 shallots
2 tbsp chinchalok *(fermented small shrimps or krill)*

Ingredients B

350 g young jackfruit, cut into bite sizes and boiled in coconut water
¼ cup shelled prawns
½ cup cooked crabmeat
100 ml coconut cream mixed with 100 ml water

Method

- Grind ingredients A into a fine paste and fry in 2–3 tbsp of oil.
- Then add in the boiled jackfruit, cooked crabmeat, and shelled prawns.
- Add in the coconut cream mixed with water and boil till cooked.
- Season to taste with salt and sugar.

5. Babi Pongteh (Peranakan Pork Stew)

This is a classic Peranakan staple that uses either pork or chicken or even both meats as in this recipe. As mentioned earlier, every household or Peranakan Baba/Nyonya has his/her own distinct way of preparing this dish – Mama Chit's old recipe is as authentic as it comes. Regardless of style, the essential ingredients are shallots, garlic paste, and preserved *taucheo* (bean paste). As with most Peranakan dishes, sambal *belachan* or fresh, raw green chillies to accompany the dish is almost mandatory.

Ingredients

600 g pork belly
200 g chicken wings or pieces of chicken
3 tbsp taucheo *(salted, fermented brown soyaa beans) paste*
2 tbsp chopped garlic
225 g shallot paste
1 tbsp ketumbar *(coriander) powder*
½ tsp dark soya sauce (be attentive to saltiness as the taucheo *may be salty)*

Method

- Fry the garlic and onions, then add the *taucheo.*
- Add the pork and fry till half cooked, then add the chicken wings, *ketumbar* powder, and the dark soya sauce.
- Pork takes about an hour to cook; alternatively, the dish can be slow-cooked in a Crockpot for about two hours.
- Serve with fresh, raw green chilli or sambal *belachan.*

6. Ayam/Itek Sio (Roast Chicken/Duck)

I have fond memories of this dish. It was typically cooked during Chinese New Year when we visited Mama Chit to pay our respects and collect *ang pows*. She would prepare the dish either using chicken or duck. Marinated in an aromatic sauce of pounded shallots, tamarind juice, and *ketumbar* (coriander seeds pounded into a powder and available in stores), the outcome, which includes the *rempah* (spice paste turned into a rich, thick sauce when cooked), is simply heavenly. Interestingly, while the term *sio* is Hokkien for 'roast', this dish is interestingly braised and fried. Using large chunks of chicken or duck when cooking the *sio*, Mama Chit would always refry the *ayam sio* and chop it into manageable pieces before serving and topping it with a generous dollop of the rich, delicious *rempah*.

Ingredients

1 whole chicken or duck, cut into large pieces
225 g shallots, ground
2 tbsp dark soya sauce
170 g tamarind, made into a paste
½ tsp pepper
3 tbsp of ketumbar *(coriander) powder*
½ tsp salt to taste
8 tbsp sugar
350 ml water

Method

- Grind shallots finely into a paste.
- Mix the tamarind with 350 ml water to form a watery paste, removing the seeds.
- Mix all ingredients together except the meat to form a paste for marinade.
- Marinate the chicken with the paste and refrigerate for at least 6 hours or overnight.
- Place the marinated chicken and juices from the marinade into a pot and cook over a large fire for 20 minutes and thereafter a low fire for another 20 minutes till the meat is tender and dry.
- Remove and cool. Before serving, fry the dish in a little oil.
- Remove and cut the meat into manageable pieces and serve with the *rempah* over the meat.

Note: Duck takes a longer time to cook; pressure-cook it for 10 minutes, then continue the process as with the chicken.

7. Peranakan Satay *Babi* (Peranakan Pork Satay)

Satay *babi*, another typical Peranakan dish, not to be confused with the traditional satay man's skewered pork on satay sticks barbecued over an open fire and accompanied with peanut sauce. This pre-war recipe, which Mum picked up from Mama Chit's elder sister Thwa Yi, uses slices of pork, preferably shoulder butt, and is another example of a spicy but drier *rempah* dish that titillates the palette. It is also one of the typical dishes served with nasi *lemak kukus*.

Ingredients

- *1½ kg pork shoulder butt*
- 600 g rempah titek *(see '*Basic Rempah*')*
- *2 tsp sugar*
- *5 slices of* lengkuas *(blue ginger)*
- *½ chicken cube*
- *4 tbsp* ketumbar *(coriander) powder*
- *½ tsp salt to taste*
- *1 stalk of* serai *(lemongrass), bruised*
- *2 kaffir lime leaves (optional)*
- *200 ml coconut milk*

Method

- Sauté all the ingredients in 2–3 tbsp of oil.
- Add the pork and coconut milk.
- Cook till tender and dry.
- Add salt and pepper to taste.

8. Sambal *Tumis* (Stir-Fried Chilli Paste)

Sambal *tumis* is a highly versatile and important sambal paste. Used as an ingredient in a dish or an accompaniment to a multitude of dishes, this old recipe combines fresh red chillies, onions, *belachan*, dried shrimp, tamarind paste, and sugar fried over a low fire until the oil separates. It makes for a wonderful accompaniment to nasi *lemak*, *lontong*, mee *rebus*, mee *siam*, or just plain rice. Also, spreading the sambal on an omelette or on top of hard-boiled egg halves as a dish (we do this as another accompaniment to nasi *lemak kukus*) or even spreading on bread with thin cucumber slices for lovely teatime sandwiches. Mum always makes sambal *tumis* in large quantity and freezes it for another occasion, which is often.

Ingredients

560 g shallots
140 g dried chilli paste
85 g belachan
56 g dried prawns, soaked and ground
225 g sugar
112 g assam *(tamarind) paste*
230 ml oil

Method

- Grind the ingredients into a fine paste and fry in 230 ml of oil.
- Add the dried prawns.
- Fry the *rempah* over gentle fire till the oil breaks (*pechah minyak*).
- Add sugar and *assam* paste (already mixed with water to make a watery mixture).

Note: This recipe is quite large in quantity. For a smaller amount, proportionately reduce the amounts, although it might be useful to prepare a sizeable quantity to freeze for future use.

9. Udang Goreng Assam (Tamarind Prawns)

This is a truly delectable and quite simple dish of fresh large prawns fried in tamarind and a dash of sugar, which produce a sweet and sourish flavour to the prawns. It is also a key accompaniment to Thwa Yi's nasi *lemak kukus*. Mum has further enhanced this dish by adding an ingredient hardly used in this dish – *hae ko* (shrimp paste). Certainly, for this dish, simplicity is the ultimate sophistication.

Ingredients

1 kg medium to large prawns
450 g assam *paste*
1 tsp salt
¼ tsp black soya sauce
5 tbsp sugar
2 tbsp hae ko *(thick prawn paste)*
60 ml water

Method

- Peel off the centre shell, leaving the head and tail intact. Clean and devein the prawns.
- Add the water to the *assam*, removing the seeds from the paste.
- Mix well the rest of the ingredients into the *assam* paste.
- Marinate the prawns with the mixed ingredients for at least an hour.
- Fry the prawns till they become brown and cooked.
- Once complete, removed onto a plate; add a little water into the wok to develop a gravy which should be thick and a little oily.
- Pour over the prawns to ensure a glaze, providing a delicious and appetising appearance.

10. Peranakan Sambal *Timun* (Peranakan Cucumber Salad)

Another of Mama Chit's old recipes, this is a fresh cucumber salad that is also a great accompaniment to nasi *lemak kukus*. Its tangy and spicy flavour serves as a palate cleanser while also being an appetiser. The Peranakans love their 'spare parts', so this recipe comes with chicken liver and gizzard, entirely optional for the more discerning.

Ingredients

250 g pork belly, boiled till cooked, then sliced into small manageable pieces
chicken liver and gizzard (optional and similarly boiled till cooked, then sliced)
1 tbsp sambal belachan
5 candlenuts, baked and smashed
juice from 5 calamansi
5 shallots, sliced finely
3 tsp fish sauce
½ bowl cilantro, chopped
3 tsp sugar
1 kaffir lime leaf, sliced finely
2 calamansi skin, sliced finely
3 tbsp dry prawns, baked and pounded
2 big cucumbers, diced (discarding the centre)

Method

- Mix all ingredients except the diced cucumber.
- Only add the cucumber into the mix when ready to serve.

11. Itek Masak Assam Cina (Tamarind Duck Chinese-Style)

A much older Peranakan woman gave this recipe to Mum before she got married. Both had enrolled in a Peranakan cooking class in Katong. Upon finding out that Mum was about to be married and having taken a liking to her, the *bibik* insisted that she note down this special recipe and cook it for her future husband. She guaranteed Mum that he would relish it. The duck cooked in a tamarind paste and using *kiam chye* (salted mustard leaves) are probably the reason why she called it *assam cina*. The dash of coconut milk added at the end enriches the flavour and texture of the dish. Mum did cook it for Pap not long after they got married, and he loved it.

Ingredients A

10 red chillies (4 fresh and 6 dry)
4 cloves of garlic
5 candlenuts
8 shallots
2 stalks of lemongrass
3 slices of blue ginger
1 tsp salt
2 tbsp brown taucheo

Ingredients B

1 duck (or chicken if you prefer), cut into bite sizes
100 g kiam chye *(thoroughly washed to reduce saltiness and sliced)*
55 g assam *(tamarind) mixed with 60 ml water to extract juice and remove seeds*
120 ml coconut milk
salt and sugar to taste

Method

- Grind ingredients A into a fine paste and fry with 3 tbsp of oil till cooked and *pechah minyak* (oil breaks).
- Add the meat to the *rempah* and fry till coated.
- Add in the *assam* juice, *kiam chye*, and a pinch of sugar to taste.
- When the meat is tender, add in the coconut milk.

Note: For a gravy or more watery consistency, add chicken stock. Also, duck takes a little longer to cook than chicken.

12. *Kueh Pulut Seri Kaya* (Coconut Custard *Kueh*)

Mum also brought Peranakan *kueh* into the household. She acquired this recipe while she was still in training at the Teachers' Training College. One of her classmates, a Peranakan girl who was always getting into all sorts of trouble, often reached out to Mum for help. Mum did so willingly without asking for anything in return, but in gratitude and knowing Mum loved cooking and baking, she gave Mum her grandmother's secret recipe for *pulut seri kaya*. Of course, Mum gladly accepted and found it to be exceptionally good.

Pulut seri kaya is a two-layered *kueh*, the bottom layer made from glutinous rice steamed in coconut milk. The Peranakans are fond of using *bunga telang* (butterfly pea flower) to randomly colour the glutinous rice. Blue food colour will also work if you want to take a shortcut. Note that for Peranakan *pulut seri kaya*, the top layer or custard is yellowish in colour, whereas the equivalent Malay *kueh* – *pulut seri muka* or *kueh salat* – has a greenish topping that comes from using the extract of crushed pandan leaves. The other difference is the absence of flour in *pulut seri kaya*. Regardless, the process requires continuous stirring to ensure the smoothness of the custard when cooking. This recipe is outstanding.

Ingredients for– *Pulut*

400 g glutinous rice
200 g coconut milk
3 pandan leaves
1 tsp salt

Method

- Soak the *pulut* for 6 hours or overnight.
- Strain the rice and add 200 g coconut milk.
- Add 1 tsp of salt and layer the rice with pandan leaves.
- Steam the rice for 20 minutes. (Check to see if cooked; if not, steam a little longer.)
- Remove the pandan leaves and transfer to a 20 × 20 cm, square tray and even out the rice.

Ingredients for *Seri Kaya*/Custard

7 large eggs (or 8 small ones)
310 g coconut cream
4 pandan leaves (knotted)
300 g sugar
½ tsp salt

Method

- o Beat eggs and mix in all ingredients.
- o Cook in a double boiler till thick. Constantly stir to ensure evenness and to prevent bubbles from forming until the mixture coats the back of a spoon.

Finishing

Pour the seri kaya over the pulut and steam over small to medium fire for 35–40 minutes. If the fire is too high, craters will form on the custard. Also, allow some steam to escape during the steaming process – this helps ensure a smooth surface on the custard. Furthermore, to ensure that the custard stays on the *pulut*, use a fork to scratch the top layer of the cooked *pulut* before pouring the custard.

13. Cathay Beef Steak

One of the recipes Mum picked up in her early married years was Cathay beef steak. This dish, served at the then iconic Cathay Restaurant, was famous. Pan-fried Cantonese-style, it is tender and succulent. Mum's sister-in-law who was then still single and living with the family had attended a cooking class from one of the former chefs at Cathay Restaurant. She was not keen on cooking but attended the class anyway. Upon completing the course, she left the printed notes strewn on the kitchen table. Being the curious person that Mum is, she casually flipped through the notes and found this recipe. Naturally, she copied it and later tried it. Without doubt, it was the real thing.

Ingredients A

1 kg beef (preferably tenderloin, cut into 1 cm thick slices)
1 tsp salt
1 tsp chicken seasoning powder
1½ tsp sugar
1 tsp sesame oil
1 tbsp oil
1 tsp bicarbonate of soda
1 egg
2 tbsp water
2 tsp Chinese wine
3 tbsp cornflour
3 tbsp light soya sauce

Ingredients B

180 ml water
1 tsp chicken seasoning powder
1½ tbsp tomato ketchup
1 tsp sesame oil
1 tsp salt
1½ tbsp sugar
3 tbsp A1 or HP Sauce

Method

- Marinate the beef with the rest of ingredients A for 2 hours.
- Mix ingredients B together to form a sauce.
- Fry the beef and add the sauce into the wok (about 2 tbsp per piece of meat).
- Serve while it's hot.

14. Pork Rolls

Knowing that she was to be married into a Cantonese household, just prior her marriage in 1956, Mum attended a cooking class taught by a Chinese lady specialising in Chinese cooking. One of her recipes has continued to appear on our dinner table from time to time. Pork rolls stuffed with ham, liver, and bamboo shoots and fried in Lea & Perrins sauce makes for a very delectable dish. The flavours emanating from the ingredients and the sauce are simply delightful.

Ingredients

500 g pork loin (big thin slices)
½ tsp sugar
½ tbsp Chinese wine
1½ tbsp dark soya sauce
1 egg
½ tsp allspice powder
15 g ham or lap cheong *(Chinese sausage)*
15 g bamboo shoots
15 g liver
2 tbsp Lea & Perrins sauce
1 tbsp tomato sauce
2 tbsp lard
1 tsp cornflour

Method

- Boil the ham, liver, and bamboo shoots and cut them into strips of about 2.5 cm long.
- Cut the meat into big thin slices and marinate with sugar, Chinese wine, soya sauce, egg, and allspice powder.
- Place a strip of ham, liver, and bamboo shoot in the centre of the meat and fold into a roll.
- Fry the rolls in lard for five minutes; sprinkle a little cornflour on either side of the rolls.
- Add the Lea & Perrins and tomato sauce, cook with the lid on for one or two minutes, and serve.

15. Peranakan *Tulang Babi* (Peranakan Pork Ribs)

At a dinner party hosted by a prominent baba who was an active promoter of Peranakan culture, he served an assortment of Peranakan dishes and *kueh* that evening. One which Mum found exceptionally good was the pork ribs cooked Peranakan-style. Quite simple in its ingredients and preparation, it is excellent when eaten with hot white rice. As he was a promoter of food and culture, he very generously shared this recipe with Mum. Enjoy!

Ingredients

500 g short pork ribs
3 tbsp rempah assam *(see 'Basic* Rempah *and Sauces')*
assam *(tamarind) water from one* assam *seed mixed with a little water*
1 stalk of lemongrass (bruised)
1 tsp sugar

Method

- Fry the *rempah* and add in the stalk of lemongrass.
- When the oil breaks, add in the pork ribs, *assam* water, and sugar.
- Cook till the meat is tender and the gravy thick.

16. Curry *Debal* (Devil Curry)

How and where Mum acquires a recipe often confounds me. This one she obtained while recuperating in hospital after a minor surgery not long after getting married. She was sharing a room, and it happened that her roommate was her brother-in-law's mother, then a much older Eurasian lady. So they got to talking about cooking and recipes – what else, right? No doubt they discussed many recipes, but this Penang-style curry *debal* is one that ranks high on Mum's list of favourites. She told Mum that she had gotten this recipe in 1947. Curry *debal* (or 'devil' in Kristang) is a spicy curry flavoured with candlenuts, chillies, coriander, turmeric, mustard seed, and vinegar from the Portuguese Eurasian Kristang culinary tradition. This dish is often prepared and served a couple of days after Christmas when there are leftovers from the Christmas fare – roast turkey, roast beef, sausages, ham, roast chicken, or whatever other meats. These all go into the pot and is cooked in *rempah* with vegetables like cabbage, cucumber, and carrots (and others if preferred). The addition of Nyonya achar adds a little zing to the dish. Again, typical of Eurasian recipes, each household has their own secret recipe. This recipe is a little milder than the fiery ones (hence *debal*) out there, but Madame De Souza's recipe is certainly a classic.

Ingredients A

1 tbsp of dried chilli paste
2 fresh red chillies
5 cm piece of ginger
15 shallots
3 cloves of garlic
8 candlenuts
1 tsp ketumbar *(coriander) powder*
1 tsp kunyit *(turmeric) powder*
1 tbsp mustard seed (pounded)

Ingredients B

4 shallots, sliced
3 cloves of garlic, sliced
2 fresh red chillies, sliced

Ingredients C

1 tbsp vinegar
1 tbsp dark soya sauce
2 tsp Colman's mustard powder
1 tsp salt

Ingredients D

1.2 kg leftover meat from Christmas fare (roast turkey, roast beef, sausages, ham, roast chicken, or whatever other meats available)
800 ml water
800 g vegetables (cabbage, cucumber, and carrots chopped in bite sizes)
200 g Nyonya achar (available in supermarkets)

Method

- Grind ingredients A into a fine paste.
- Mix ingredients C together.
- Fry the sliced ingredients B, then add the ground ingredients A.
- Add the meats, then the mixed ingredients C.
- Continue frying to properly coat the meats with the *rempah*.
- Add the water and bring to a boil.
- Add in the vegetables and cook for another 8–10 minutes.
- Finally, add the achar and adjust salt and sugar seasoning according to taste.
- Serve with white rice or French loaf.

COMFORT FOOD FOR THE KIDS

I grew up in a home where my paternal grandmother, Mama, had employed a domestic helper from China as far back as the 1930s. She came from a specific group of women from a district in Kwangtung (Guangdong) Province who took a vow of celibacy and never to marry. They were respectfully known as *majie* (*ma cheh* in Cantonese) or black-and-white amah. You could identify them by their traditional attire of black trousers and white blouse, wearing their hair in a bun. The attributes of the *ma cheh* such as loyalty, honesty, and skills in cooking and babysitting were highly regarded. Many worked for their employers till a ripe old age.

Ours was affectionately known as Hau Cheh or elder sister Hau. Hau Cheh was devoted and loyal to the family for over fifty years, finally retiring to her hometown in Kwangtung in the late 1980s. Interestingly, it was at a time when I had my firstborn, and we had engaged a Filipino helper. Although Hau Cheh wanted to continue the tradition of helping raise the third generation, she was really getting on in age and refused help. Sadly, it all came to a head when words were exchanged, and the family insisted on providing the help. She very quickly decided then that it was time to move on.

You see, she helped raise my father, the eldest son, and his two sisters, followed by us, his children – my elder brother, Tony; younger sister, Daphne; and myself. She was family, and it was a sad day when she decided to return home to China and even sadder the manner in which she left – within a day after more than fifty years. In retrospect and in trying to understand the mindset of the very loyal *ma cheh*, it had to be a grievous event to occur before they could part ways with the family they served. She had often spoken about returning home, so I believe the disagreement was dramatic enough and an ideal justification in her mind to finally call it a day. And leaving within a day was symbolic of cleanly severing ties. I found it difficult to understand then, but the bonds of loyalty that came from a distant past and now defunct *ma cheh* culture probably explains her behaviour and actions. It also convinces me that this no longer exists in our modern-day society. We never heard from Hau Cheh again.

Of course, one of the things we remember her best for was her culinary skills. She was a fantastic cook, and I am sure she initially obtained recipes through exchange within her *ma cheh* network. Nonetheless, for the duration of her many years living in Singapore, she had also developed recipes on her own and prepared dishes for us that adopted local spices suited to local taste buds. Her repertoire of recipes was wide, but the truly amazing thing was that they were never written down and were all drawn from memory.

Mum, who married into my father's home, had over the years hounded and observed Hau Cheh attentively and had to use all means to obtain her recipes. One tactic which worked was telling her that I was going away to university in Canada and needed them to survive! Mum did successfully manage to collect many of Hau Cheh's best recipes and unashamedly also learnt a thing or two from her. Growing up through my teenage years (and I had a voracious appetite then), I count many of these dishes as comfort food, some simple and easy to prepare but all eliciting very nostalgic and pleasant memories for me.

1. Sweet and Sour Pork

Hau Cheh's recipe, unlike many other sweet and sour pork recipes, is done in a style that requires some labour of love. In other words, it takes a little more time and effort. The meat is bruised, tenderised, marinated, and compressed into a ball before frying. The outcome is a delicious and succulent pork ball that when accompanied with the sweet and sour sauce makes for a very delectable dish. She would prepare this dish mostly at dinner time and usually quite a lot as my brother and I would wolf down significant quantities of it.

Ingredients A

1 kg pork (shoulder butt), makes about 50 balls
2 tbsp light soya sauce
2 tbsp Chinese wine
¼ tsp pepper
1 tsp of chicken seasoning powder
1 egg
1 tbsp cake flour

Ingredients B

1 tbsp minced garlic
1 tbsp Lingham's chilli sauce
2 tbsp light soya sauce
1 tbsp sesame oil
2 tbsp tomato sauce
½ cup water
½ tbsp potato flour

Method

- Cut the pork into strips and tenderise with a mallet.
- Marinate the meat with the rest of ingredients A for half an hour.
- Shape the meat into 4 cm balls.
- Roll the pork balls in a mixture of 2 tbsp cake flour and 2 tbsp potato flour.
- Deep-fry the pork balls till cooked and crispy and set aside.
- For the sauce, fry the garlic, then add the rest of ingredients B. Cook till sauce is thick.
- Place the balls into the sauce and fry till sauce coats the balls.

2. *Babi Hancur* (Minced Pork and Diced Potatoes)

Hancur means 'destroy' or 'crush'. Nothing so dramatic here; what it actually describes is a minced pork dish, one that is simple and fairly easy to prepare. The original recipe came from Mum's mother, Mama Chit. Hau Cheh made an excellent *babi hancur*. Served with steaming white rice, I enjoy it when accompanied with sambal *belachan* and dark soya sauce. Wow!

Ingredients

600 g minced pork
300 g potato, diced into 1 cm cubes and soaked in water
3 shallots, sliced
¼ tsp black pepper
1 big white onion, sliced
2 eggs
½ tbsp light soya sauce

Method

- Marinate the minced pork with 1 egg and light soya sauce.
- Drain and dry the diced potato, fry till brown, and set aside.
- Fry the shallots and big onion and add the minced meat. Fry till cooked.
- Add in the fried potatoes and 1 egg.
- Drizzle light and dark soya sauce and sprinkle with pepper.

3. Lor Mai Fun (Glutinous Rice)

One of my personal favourites, this is a recipe from my paternal grandmother, Mama. Today I enjoy not only eating this savoury dish but also cooking it. It is a flexible recipe in that there are basic ingredients, but as a home-cooked dish, one can be generous and add a lot more goodies that enhance the overall flavour and give the dish more oomph. It is fantastic as a breakfast meal, but it can be eaten any time of the da, and I do. By the way, whenever I prepare this dish, I usually make a little extra to share with my golf buddies during a game. One of them whose father would buy *lor mai fun* every Sunday morning from the market similarly calls it a comfort food, and upon tasting it the very first time, he said it brought tears to his eyes!

Ingredients A

800 g glutinous rice (soaked for 3 hours, then drained)
6 shallots, sliced
1 strip of lap yoke *(Chinese cured pork belly), diced*
2 lap cheong *(Chinese waxed sausage), diced*
5 dried shiitake mushrooms, rehydrated and diced
120 g ground nuts (boiled for 25 minutes), much easier to use boiled canned ground nuts
100 g dried prawns, soaked, then drained

Ingredients B

1 tsp dark soya sauce
2 tbsp light soya sauce
1 chicken seasoning cube
1 tsp of Knorr Hao Chi seasoning powder
1 tsp salt
1 tsp sesame oil
2 tsp oyster sauce
1 tsp five-spice powder

Garnish

2 tbsp fried shallots
2 stalks of spring onions, chopped

Method

- Using 2 tbsp of oil, fry the shallots, then the remainder of ingredients A except rice. Set aside.
- In the same wok, add 1 tbsp of oil and fry the rice with ingredients B.
- Return ingredients A into the work and mix evenly into the rice.
- Remove the rice and place in a steamer, add 400 ml water and steam for 20–30 minutes. Check if the rice is cooked and no longer grainy.
- When cooked, remove and garnish with spring onions and fried shallots.

4. Stir-Fried Mustard Greens with Seafood and Sliced Pork

A mishmash of salted vegetables, seafood, and pork, this stir-fried dish is the perfect pair with steaming white rice. Flavourful and a little tangy from the mustard greens and tomatoes, the combination with seafood and meat makes for a well-balanced dish. It's another one of those dishes that evoke emotions and happy memories of a bygone childhood.

Ingredients

100 g salted mustard greens, scalded, squeezed dry, and cut in 2 cm squares
100 g pork, sliced into bite sizes
80 g pork liver, sliced into bite sizes
1 sotong (squid), sliced into bite sizes
1 large tomato, cut into wedges
1 capsicum, cut into bite sizes
½ tsp garlic paste
5 slices of ginger
½ tsp light soya sauce
½ tsp sugar
1 tsp cornflour

Method

- Fry the garlic paste and ginger.
- Add in the pork, liver, sotong, tomatoes, capsicum, and salted vegetables.
- Make a slurry using the cornflour and water and add in to thicken the gravy.
- Finally, add light soya sauce and sugar to taste.

5. Macaroni and Sausages

This is another simple dish that I would look forward to when coming home for lunch after school. Admittedly, I ate copious amounts of this as it was so easy to devour. I suspect kids everywhere will enjoy this dish. I certainly did as do my kids even when they were growing up. In fact, it is still a well-loved dish on our lunch or dinner table today, and it remains a popular quick one-dish meal for the family when constrained by time.

Ingredients

400 g boiled macaroni
2 sausages, sliced
4 rashes of bacon, sliced
3 eggs
2 tbsp butter
1 big white onion, sliced
1 tbsp oil
2 tbsp dark soya sauce
2 tsp light soya sauce
½ tsp white pepper
½ cup cheddar cheese
¼ cup chopped cilantro
2 tbsp fried shallots

Method

- Fry the big onion, bacon, and sausages in butter and oil.
- Add in the macaroni and continue frying.
- Add 3 eggs and fry till well mixed.
- Add the light and dark soya sauce.
- When done, remove and mix in the cheddar cheese.
- Garnish with cilantro, fried shallots, and white pepper.

6. Chuen Kuen (Spring Rolls)

Chuen kuen is a traditional dish I always looked forward to during the Chinese New Year season. It is another of Hau Cheh's recipes which again brings back happy memories, especially of our reunion dinner on Lunar Chinese New Year's Eve, when immediate and extended family on Pap's side would gather. Of course, there were numerous other traditional dishes she would prepare, such as *ho see fatt choy, pak cham kai, pau yue wong ah pak*, etc. but *chuen kuen* was certainly one I was very fond of. Do note the Cantonese influence when I was growing up as my paternal grandmother and Hau Cheh were, of course, Cantonese. With the passing of time and older folk, I guess we've lost quite a lot of the Cantonese traditions/influences, save for the food. It has never been the same again at Chinese New Year, for me at least, not much like my childhood and teenage years, but c'est la vie, and traditions evolve.

Ingredients

500 g minced pork
1 piece chopped liver
10 water chestnuts, minced
100 g prawn meat, minced
½ tsp cornflour
¼ tsp pepper
½ tsp salt
1 tsp five-spice powder
100 g crabmeat
½ tsp sugar
½ tsp chicken seasoning powder

Additional Ingredients

Tofu skins, cut into 15 × 15 cm square (wipe with a wet cloth to remove salt)

Method

- Mix all ingredients together.
- Wrap ingredients in the tofu skins as you would *popiah* (spring rolls).
- Tie the *chuen kuen* with raffia in a blanket stitch, then steam for 15–20 minutes.
- Remove the *chuen kuen* and raffia and allow to cool.
- Finally, fry till crisp and golden brown.

7. Sar Poh Kai (Clay Pot Chicken)

Here is yet another favoured dish that Hau Cheh would prepare in large portions for dinner and one that I would look forward as leftovers for lunch after school (if there was any left in the first place). It is best cooked in a clay pot and ingredients such as red dates, goji berries, ginseng, orange peel, and other goodies cooked together with the chicken marinated in various sauces, producing a flavourful and aromatic chicken dish that is simply to die for.

Ingredients (A)

4 chicken thighs, cut into bite sizes
orange peel from half an orange
2 pieces of tong kwai *(angelica root)*
5 ang cho *(red dates)*
1 tbsp goji berry
2 lap cheong *(waxed Chinese sausages), cut into 2.5 cm length*
5 pieces black mushrooms, soaked, cleaned, and cut into quarters
1 whole carrot, sliced into florets or carrot flowers

Ingredients B

2 tbsp oyster sauce
½ tsp fish sauce
½ tbsp light soya sauce
¼ tsp dark soya sauce
2 tsp ginger juice
1 tbsp Chinese wine
1 cube of chicken seasoning
1 tsp potato flour

Method

- Marinate the chicken with ingredients B.
- Fry the mushrooms and *lap cheong* in 2 tbsp oil. Remove and set aside.
- Fry the chicken in 3 tbsp oil, then add the orange peel, *ang cho*, goji berries, and *tong kwai.*
- Remove all and place in a clay pot or Crockpot, add ½ cup water and bring to a boil.
- When chicken is almost cooked, add in carrots, mushrooms, and *lap cheong* and adjust salt and sugar seasoning to taste. Gravy is thick and flavourful.

8. Hau Cheh's Salt Fish Achar (Salt Fish Pickle)

Achar is a favourite pickle appetiser that is enjoyed amongst the peoples of Southeast Asia and India. Obviously, there are varying differences in style, preparation, ingredients, and even spiciness. Regardless of whether it is Peranakan, Malay, Indian, or Eurasian, the common factor is the pickling process. We're not sure where Hau Cheh got this recipe from, but there seems to be a fusion of styles here. She pickled using vinegar, which not only affects the food's texture and flavour but also preserves and extends the shelf life of this appetiser. A simple but very mouth-watering achar, the recipe uses salted fish and lots of sinful fried crispy pork lard.

Ingredients A

1 tsp dried chilli paste
2.5 cm of turmeric, sliced
3 candlenuts
15 g belachan

Ingredients B

2.5 cm of ginger, sliced
4 shallots, sliced
2 cloves of garlic, smashed

Ingredients C

85 g salted fish (scalded, washed, and sliced into ½ cm thick)
6 tbsp water
2 tbsp white vinegar
50 g sugar
120 g fried crispy pork lard

Method

- Grind ingredients A into a fine paste.
- Fry the salted fish till crisp, then set aside.
- Fry ingredients B, then add Ingredients A, and fry till fragrant.
- Add the water, vinegar, and sugar, followed by the fried salted fish.
- Finally, add in the crispy pork lard.

9. Black Mee *Siam* (Black Siamese Noodles)

Credit goes to my paternal grandmother, Mama, for this unusual mee *siam* recipe. Mee *siam* originated in northern Malaysia and is called such as its flavour is reminiscent of Thai cuisine. This recipe is quite unlike most Nyonya mee *siam* recipes which typically use tamarind, *belachan*, and *taucheo* that bring out a strong but balanced sweet-sour flavour. Mum's favourite Nyonya mee *siam* recipe can be found in pg ... However, this black mee *siam* recipe which I often refer to as a Cantonese-style mee *siam*, uses only black and brown *taucheo* and soya sauce. The gravy ends up being black instead of the reddish hue of the typical mee *siam*. Using the same accompaniments such as prawns, boiled eggs, *ku chai* (garlic chives), etc. it is less tangy than the Nyonya version but no less tasty. This one-dish meal is a favourite of my eldest son, Christopher, which I guess proves that comfort food is often passed down from generation to generation.

Ingredients A

1 tbsp dried chilli paste
10 shallots
¼ tsp salt

Ingredients B

5 calamansi
½ tsp light soya sauce
160 g black taucheo
40 g brown taucheo
2–3 tbsp sugar
250 g shallots
1 litre water
500 ml prawn stock
1 cube of chicken seasoning

Ingredients C

450 g bee hoon
300 g taugeh *(bean sprouts)*
600 g prawns

Garnish

Boiled prawns
4–5 boiled eggs, sliced in half
½ cup of ku chai
3 tau pok, *cut into small cubes*

Method
Noodles

- Grind ingredients A into a fine paste.
- Boil the prawns, de-shell, and continue to boil the shells to make 500 ml of prawn stock.
- Fry the ground ingredients A, adding salt. Save 1 tbsp paste for the prawns.

- Fry the cooked prawns with the saved 1 tbsp paste.
- Scald the *bee hoon* and *taugeh* and mix in the remainder of the paste. Mix evenly and add a touch of light soya sauce to taste.

Gravy

- Grind 250 g shallots, then mix in the black and brown *taucheo.*
- Using 2 tbsp oil, fry the mixture, then add 1,000 ml water and 500 ml prawn stock.
- Add the cube of chicken seasoning and sugar to taste.

Finishing

- When serving, place the noodles in a deep plate and garnish with prawns, slices of egg, sprinkling of *tau pok*, and *ku chye.*
- Pour gravy generously over the mee *siam* and add a blob of sambal *tumis.*

10. Bread Patties

This old and unusual recipe which I fondly recall from my growing up years had evolved from post-war years when bread was again plentiful. It was as if, after being deprived of it for so long, when it was readily available again, people went crazy and just bought a lot of bread. Ultimately, there would be an excess of leftover bread, which could be repurposed, for example, into Parsi bread pudding or, in this instance, a fried patty. This recipe includes a tasty *lap cheong* (Chinese sausage) filling, fried like a pancake. It was a fantastic teatime snack that I would wolf down when I came home from school after playing football or athletics, and I would lose count of how many I ate. I did often get scolded by Hau Cheh for eating too many and for fear of spoiling dinner. But when dinner rolled around, it was off to the races again!

Ingredients

2 lap cheong (Chinese waxed sausage), chopped into small cubes
100 g dried prawns, soaked and drained
1 egg, beaten lightly
3 shallots, sliced
2 tsp sago flour
10 slices of bread, crust removed
½ tsp five-spice powder
¼ tsp salt
¼ tsp pepper

Method

- Soak the bread in water, mash, then squeeze dry.
- Fry the shallots in 2 tbsp of oil, then add the diced *lap cheong* and dry prawns.
- Add five-spice powder and salt and pepper to taste, then remove to cool.
- Mix the egg and flour into the mashed bread, then add the fried ingredients and mix well.
- Make into patties and shallow-fry.
- Serve with Lingham's chilli sauce or tomato ketchup.

11. Hamburger

Some readers may recall Jackie's Bowl (later Orchard Bowl) at Cathay's Orchard Cinema, where an excellent hamburger was served at the counter of the bowling alley. This would have been in the early 1970s, and the proprietor of the catering service was the father of my old school chum John, who sadly is now deceased. John was also close to my family and became a godson to my parents when he converted to Catholicism. We spent many outings at Jackie's Bowl in our younger days and without fail would always devour hamburgers in between bowling. We raved over the hamburger, and Mum couldn't resist trying it too. Mum tasted the hamburger, and she had to get the recipe. Rather than approach John's father, she gave her godson the mission of commandeering the recipe for her. John delivered. The patties include a range of ingredients that after frying and placing in between hamburger buns together with onions, tomatoes, lettuce, mustard, and relish is simply delicious. We would get this occasionally at lunch when John would come by, and he swore it tasted just like his dad's. Thanks, John.

Ingredients

450 g minced beef (makes 6 patties)
2 cloves of garlic, chopped
2 large white onions, chopped
2 slices of toast bread, mashed
2 eggs
¼ cup chopped cilantro
¼ tsp pepper
¼ tsp salt
¼ tsp Colman's mustard

Method

- Mix all Ingredients well into the minced beef.
- Form patties, fry, and serve between hamburger buns with raw onions, tomatoes, and lettuce.

12. Nyonya Macaroni Soup

This is another of Mama Chit's old Nyonya recipes. Simple in preparation yet so tasty, I grew up with this dish, and today it's still a comfort food for me. It's really a home-made chicken soup over macaroni and garnished with croutons, fried shallots, chopped spring onions, fresh red chillies, and cilantro. Of course, the chicken soup is tasty, but what makes it for me is the garnishing that brings forth that extra zing, especially the home-made croutons. Typically, if there was macaroni left over, we would fry it with sausages the next day (recipe also found in this chapter) and turn it into another comfort dish.

Ingredients

1 chicken or 650 g chicken parts
400 g packet of elbow macaroni
½ nutmeg seed
6 cm cinnamon bark
½ tsp peppercorn
5 cloves
3 litres water
¼ tsp salt

Garnish

½ cup croutons
½ cup fried shallots
½ cup spring onions, chopped
½ cup cilantro, chopped
2 fresh red chillies, sliced

Method

- Boil the macaroni till cooked.
- Boil the chicken in 3 litres of water, adding in all ingredients.
- When cooked, remove the chicken and shred.
- Serve the macaroni with shredded chicken and soup, adding the garnish.

13. Pork Trotters Cantonese-Style

Hau Cheh was utterly amazing in that she was able to cook so many delicious dishes and all from memory including ingredients, proportions, and method. I imagine that this was a gift or talent that you find similarly with gifted pianists who play only by ear and melody, unable to read a single note of music. That all her dishes could be replicated in taste and appearance every time was further testimony to her talent. This dish was one of her specialties, and it takes time to prepare and cook pork trotters, preferably front hooves for its tendons and muscles and certainly for the taste and collagen. Using a slow cooker or Crockpot enables the cooking and simmering of the meat with the advantage of unattended cooking for many hours, which can be spent doing other things. When ready, serve the trotters on top of a bed of pickled cucumber slices. It is mouth-watering, and we enjoy it with chicken rice chilli sauce.

Ingredients A

1 tbsp tausi *(black beans)*
2 tbsp brown taucheo *paste*
1 tbsp garlic paste
1 tbsp sugar
1 cube of chicken seasoning
½ tsp dark soya sauce
2 tbsp cake flour
350 ml water

Ingredients B

2 pork trotters (front leg recommended)
pickled cucumber – 250 g cucumber, 1 tsp salt, 2 tsp white vinegar, and 1 tbsp sugar

Method

- Cut the cucumber in thin slices, add salt, and mix well. Then add sugar and white vinegar to the cucumber and stir to blend well. Pickle for an hour.
- Blanch the trotters – put in cold water and bring to a boil to cleanse the meat. Remove and dry when done.
- Rub the trotters with cake flour.
- Fry ingredients A, then add in the trotters.
- Add in the water, place in a Crockpot, and let it cook for 3 hours on high.
- When ready, serve the trotters and thick gravy on a bed of pickled cucumber slices.

THE WORKING YEARS

Both my parents had long careers in civil service, you might say from cradle to grave. It was just the way things were then; you didn't jump about, and you worked hard and rose through the ranks if you had the ability and ambition to do so. Mum was quite happy being a primary school teacher and was more supportive of Pap's career than her own. She even decided not to pursue the principal track when offered the chance to do so. She recognised that raising her three children with no domestic help in those days, teaching and preparing for classes, cooking meals, and attending to Pap as well as accompanying him to police events, often also cooking for his meetings, didn't leave her much time to grow in her career. Pap was proud of his wife's culinary skills and would often bring food to meetings and events which was always a big hit. Nevertheless, she had no regrets about her own career and felt she gained much more being by his side.

Mum joined the Teachers' Training College in 1952. After qualifying, she had postings to several primary schools over the years – Waterloo Girl's School, Balestier Primary, Raffles Girls' School, Toa Payoh Primary, Cairnhill Primary, and finally Catholic High School – before she retired in 1984. She specialised in teaching children from primary 1 to 6, and many of her students rose to be very successful in their chosen careers and till this day remember her as a caring, inspiring, and dedicated teacher. She takes great pride in having touched so many lives and seeing them flourish, especially the children who came from broken homes and were often in need. She counts these and the family she brought up as her greatest achievements.

When she met Pap, he was already a police inspector. She was introduced to him via a double date by a close fellow teacher and friend who herself was already married to a police inspector. For Mum, those were wonderful, carefree days including their early marriage years from 1956 right through to Britain granting Singapore self-government in 1959. Tough, troubling years followed when Singapore was finding its feet with a new local government, followed by Singapore's merger with Malaysia in 1963 and finally emerging a republic in 1965. She remembers the austerity drive in the civil service where the government removed what was then a cost-of-living allowance almost equal to the salary. Already with two children in tow and with half of what they typically earned, they had to cut expenses. Pap went with a crew cut, Mum sewed her own clothes, and they didn't go out much – pretty much a no-frills lifestyle for some years. It was during these years that Pap's career started to evolve.

The 1950s saw him posted back and forth to various police stations like Kandang Kerbau and Paya Lebar and the Criminal Investigation Department for a few years during a time when riots such as the Hock Lee bus and Chinese student riots were commonplace. Union strikes also started to emerge, and it was at this time that Pap was appointed and given command of the newly formed D Troop in the then reserve unit. They were specially trained in dealing with illegal strikes and were located at the former Hill Street Police Station. It was probably this posting and his experience at CID that led to his next job in Special Branch (Internal Security Department today). His then boss was George Bogaars, the first Singaporean to head Special Branch. Being an administrative service civil servant and non-police officer appointed to head and revamp the unit, Mr Bogaars needed trained police officers to assist him, and Pap was one of a number who were later recruited into the Branch. This was a turbulent time as the communist threat of infiltrating trade unions and schools was causing unrest, strikes, and even riots.

One of the most prominent operations of the time was Operation Coldstore in early 1963. This operation led to over a hundred arrests of suspected communists and effectively crippled the communist threat in Singapore. Trained in interrogation, one of Pap's tasks after their incarceration was to assess, rehabilitate, and ensure that they recant their ideological beliefs before being permitted to rejoin society. It was during this process that the family was directly affected. The strategy called for the political detainees who were by then already somewhat rehabilitated to move into a halfway house, and Pap would spend time with them in the evenings to assess their readiness to return to mainstream society. The halfway house was a large black and white bungalow with a large garden in quiet Mount Rosie Road. The family occupied half the bungalow, and the other half was occupied by at least five or six political detainees at any one time. After a period and after they were assessed to be ready, they would officially recant and then leave the house thereafter. Pap was also involved with resettling them back into society with jobs and aftercare.

Pap had a job to do, and we were too young to understand its implications. All I knew as a child then with zero political understanding was that the detainees were very nice people who taught me how to play volleyball. They were mostly professional – a doctor, lawyers, and some businessmen. Living there probably disrupted our family from an adult's point of view as Mama, Hau Cheh, and one of Pap's sisters were all part of the family and living together. But I must admit, though, that having had the rare privilege of living in a large colonial black and white bungalow not only brings back fond memories whenever I see one but also has ever since piqued my interest in them and the lifestyle of those who occupied them back in a distant time.

We occupied the colonial bungalow from 1965 to 1972, when a change in leadership at ISD led to Pap's leaving and to a new posting as controller of immigration. Immigration was completely new to him, but he took it in his stride and learnt the trade. He enjoyed the experience and always thought highly of the people working there. When his three-year posting was up, Pap went back to his beloved police force as assistant commissioner and head of CID.

This move pretty much grounded him and brought him back to real policing and dealing with the negative elements of society. Hardcore triads and secret societies were rampant and, in many instances, even violent in the 1960s and 1970s. Having had to deal with them in the late '50s and early '60s, he was again involved with dismantling many of these gangs when he returned to CID a decade later, this time as its head. It was only in the 1990s that this dangerous and menacing threat to society was successfully supressed, although one wonders if they will ever truly be eradicated.

Whilst Pap was at CID, the Singapore government had decided that the then Paya Lebar Airport would no longer be able to cope with the growing traffic. Hence, they approved the building of a brand-spanking-new Changi Airport in 1975, which would also facilitate expansion in the coming decades. Hence, the preparation and initial groundwork began.

With his exposure to immigration and many years in security, Pap was understandably tasked to lead the initial study and design of airport security and immigration checkpoints. This mandate led him to travel and visit the many larger and more sophisticated airports around the world to learn and then implement what would work best for Singapore. Mum had the opportunity to accompany him on some of those trips.

He spent five years at CID before being promoted to deputy commissioner where he served another five years, seeing through the completion of the Changi Airport project. He was one of the last non-university graduates to occupy the deputy commissioner position, and after thirty-two years in the service, Pap retired from the police force in 1984 with a full pension (no longer the practice today). He did continue to work for six years after, serving as the executive director of the Singapore Manufacturers' Association (SMA) before fully retiring in 1990.

On a personal note, Pap was a loving and supportive father, a fiercely loyal man to his family, friends, country, and the police force. He was religious and a serious, hard-working, straight-talking, no-nonsense man who did have a sense of humour, albeit sparingly. He was a sizeable man (six feet two inches tall and weighing 230 pounds in his heyday) with a strong, imposing presence. He possessed a short fuse and demanded much from his family and colleagues, although at most times not unreasonably so. But he did have a soft spot and would readily and genuinely help people in need and would go out of his way to do so if he assessed them to be sincere.

He raised us very strictly when we were growing up in the 1970s as he was very much aware of the hazards on the streets, which were then flooded with easily attainable drugs and the negative influences of secret societies on youth. Even as an 18-year-old, I had to ask permission to go to a party a week ahead of time, complete with the drilling questions of who and where and being told of the time to come home. He would still be up to ensure that the agreed timing was adhered to. However, I do recall fondly and with much appreciation that, even as a senior officer with a busy schedule, Pap who was a former sportsman would make time to support my sporting achievements in school, coming to watch me play football or compete in athletics. He also enjoyed his armchair football and was loyal to his favourite team, Liverpool. I enjoy the same pastime except my team is Arsenal.

His supportive efforts would later extend to every Sunday evening for many months, taking a long drive to Jurong to send my two buddies and me back to SAFTI Military Institute when we were in Officer Cadet School. After I completed my national service, the support continued with my tertiary education in

Canada (and my sister in the United States), which I later learnt was burdensome as I experienced the same when supporting my sons through their overseas education. It was a hefty effort to support two kids abroad at university at the time, so Mum made and sold cakes to supplement their income. She supplied a cake shop with chocolate fudge cakes, peach chiffon cakes, and a variety of tarts until we graduated.

I will admit that Pap was a very strong influence on me as far as family, values, career, and work ethic are concerned. Of course, Mum is pleased that I have shared Pap's résumé here, even though she and her favourite recipes are the focal point of the book. After all, Mum did devote much of her life mainly to him including cooking, hence our dedication of this book to Pap.

1. Chocolate Fudge Cake

Mum was always interested in baking and desserts and delved deeply into it in the 1960s. Around the mid-sixties, the rage in town was the very successful Lana chocolate fudge cake. It was and still is very good. However, Mum wanted to bake the cake as good as Lana's and made it a personal challenge. She knew that she was never ever going to get the original recipe, so she tried to get as close to it as possible by using other chocolate fudge recipes and experimenting. She was so obsessed that she baked it twenty-seven times on the trot to get close to perfection. I ate a whole lot of chocolate cake then until it came out of my ears!

She finally struck gold on the twenty-seventh attempt and has kept to the same recipe ever since. Of course, many have tried her chocolate fudge cake, and George Bogaars, who recruited Pap into ISD in the early '60s, loved it. After he left ISD, George would still get together with some of his ISD foodie *kakis* once a month or so in the late '60s and early '70s. They would pig out at different places, even at roadside food stalls if the food was good. He always insisted that Pap bring one of Mum's chocolate fudge cakes for dessert, and he would literally reserve half for himself! Mum's recipe rivals the original chocolate fudge cake from Lana Cakes, which today I believe has also evolved. But if you recall eating the original cake – some have said that Mum's version is as good or even better – then try this recipe for yourself, and you be the judge.

Ingredients for Cake

6 eggs
180 ml water
*85 g cake flour**
½ tsp baking soda
½ tsp baking powder
¼ tsp salt
1 tsp vanilla essence
70 g butter, melted
3 tbsp chocolate paste
120 ml rum
½ tsp lemon juice
60 g dark chocolate, melted
2 tbsp of evaporated milk
½ tsp cream of tartar
140 g sugar

**Betty Crocker's SoftaSilk cake flour is recommended. If not available, use Prima Top flour.*

Method

- Separate the egg yolks from the whites.
- Mix thoroughly the water, evaporated milk, melted butter, chocolate paste, rum, vanilla essence, lemon juice, and melted dark chocolate (1).
- Sift the flour, baking powder, baking soda, and salt together. Sift three times to ensure no lumps, making it lighter and easier to mix into other ingredients (2).

- Beat the egg yolks with 60 g sugar for 10–12 minutes at high speed.
- Separately in a clean bowl, beat the egg whites with 80 g sugar and ½ tsp cream of tartar for 3 minutes at high speed, taking care not to overbeat.
- Add (1) and (2) into the egg yolk mixture and stir well.
- Add a scoop of the egg whites into the egg yolk mixture and mix gently.
- Pour the entire egg yolk mixture into the remainder of the egg whites and use your hands to mix in lightly and deftly.
- Pour the entire mixture into an *ungreased and clean* cake pan and bake at 150°C for 30–35 minutes.
- When the cake is cooked, invert the cake pan and cool upside down in the pan as the spongy structure hasn't set. When cold, the cake is ready for the fudge icing.

Ingredients for Fudge Topping/Icing

60 g dark chocolate
475 ml water
60 g sugar
3 tsp instant jelly
½ tsp rum
½ tsp vanilla
1½ tbsp chocolate paste
1 tbsp butter
2 tbsp hoon kueh *(mung bean) flour*
2 tsp custard powder
½ tsp salt

Method

- Mix the flour and custard with some water to make a paste.
- Place the instant jelly, chocolate, chocolate paste, vanilla, rum, and salt into the 475 ml water and boil.
- When boiling, slowly add in the flour mixture.
- Continue cooking till mixture is thick, then add the butter to give the fudge a shine.

Finishing

- While still warm, immediately ice the cake, which may be sliced in half for a two-layered cake.
- Apply fudge over the bottom half and then all over the cake when reassembled.

2. Breudher Cake

The late George Bogaars, who was a firm foodie, loved Mum's chocolate fudge cake. It was probably because he had requested for it on so many of his eat-out sessions with the *kakis* that he perhaps felt compelled to share an old family recipe with her. In fact, Mum suspected that he wanted her to bake it for him; she did, and he was thrilled with the outcome. George was born and bred in Singapore, and his heritage was Ceylonese (now Sri Lanka) Dutch Burgher. Since the sixteenth century, there was significant Dutch influence in Southeast Asia, mostly in Indonesia and Malaysia but also in Ceylon, where many moved to Singapore in the late nineteenth century. Breudher is a typical Dutch Eurasian recipe which can be found across the region, all named slightly differently. It is essentially a buttery yeast cake that is traditionally made at Christmastime. A cross between a cake and a bread, it is often a closely guarded family secret with some variations to each family's recipe, very much like the Eurasian *sugee* cake. He was a generous man, so I'm sure George wouldn't mind us sharing this lovely Dutch-influenced recipe. He did also share one other family recipe that follows.

Ingredients

75 ml water
1 tsp yeast
115 g flour
115 g butter
140 g sugar
12 egg yolks
1 tsp vanilla essence
3 drops of rose essence
140 g flour
1 tsp baking powder

Method

- Dissolve 1 tsp yeast into 75 ml water, then add 115 g flour and allow to ferment for 1½ hours.
- Whisk butter with the sugar, adding the vanilla and rose essence.
- When smooth and white, add in the egg yolks and continue whisking till well mixed.
- Lastly, fold in 140 g flour and baking powder.
- Place the mixture in a greased pan and let it rest for 4 hours.
- Bake for 40–45 minutes at 160°C.

3. Homemade Mayonnaise

George was proud of this recipe and actually called it mayonnaise à la Bogaars, handwritten on a piece of paper that Mum still keeps. The ingredients and method of preparation are quite elaborate, and while you can buy mayonnaise easily off the shelf, I guess there is something about home-made recipes that brings forth a sense of satisfaction and pride, especially when it is a little different from those you find on the shelf.

Ingredients

4 egg yolks
3 tbsp olive oil
1 tbsp malt vinegar
½ large white onion
¼ tsp finely ground pepper

Method

- Slice and soak the onion in the vinegar for 2–3 hours (for flavour only).
- Whisk the egg yolks in a mixer very slowly for 25–30 minutes.
- Drip the olive oil into the mixer drop by drop.
- When done, drip the vinegar into the mixture in a similar fashion.
- Add a dash of finely ground pepper and continue mixing till blended.

The following two recipes come with an amusing story that involves one of Singapore's founding fathers, Dr Goh Keng Swee. This would be sometime in the mid-sixties when he was then minister for the interior and defence. There was an important meeting at ISD, and Pap, as usual, planned for a tea break, arranging for Mum to make some of her *kueh-kueh*. It was well known that Dr Goh, a Malacca-born Peranakan, loved his *kueh-kueh*. There was trepidation at the onset of the meeting as he arrived in a foul mood, probably from the last meeting that had not gone well. Upon arrival, when he glanced at the side table where all the goodies were laid out, his mood immediately changed. Not only did the meeting go well but he also had his secretary cancel a lunch appointment, saying he was staying for lunch. Pap's colleagues later thanked Mum profusely for having changed Dr Goh's mood and saving the day with the goodies she provided, which resulted in a successful meeting and prevented the proverbial rolling heads. We will share two of the recipes that was on the table that day – *talam keladi* (steamed yam tray cake) and *susi* buns (Eurasian savoury meat bun).

4. Kueh Talam Keladi (Yam Tray Cake)

Kueh talam keladi is made primarily from yam. It is a typical Peranakan *kueh* or dessert which in most traditions is eaten after the main meal. However, the Peranakans will eat their *kueh-kueh* any time of the day and sometimes even making it their main meal. *Talam keladi*, not so commonly found today, is a two-layered *kueh* that is steamed and presented in a beautiful purple and white layer. The springy texture and the flavours of yam and pandan is delicious; the purple yam portion is the base, and the top white portion is made from coconut cream and flour. I am told this *kueh* was what initially got Dr Goh excited.

Ingredients for Yam Base

350 g yam – to get a grated weight of 300 g
2 tbsp cornstarch
100 ml coconut milk
1 tbsp rice flour
¼ tsp salt
4 tbsp sugar
4 drops of purple colouring

Method

- Peel, wash (getting rid of the slime), and grate the yam.
- Add water to the grated yam in a muslin cloth and squeeze dry to get 300 g grated yam
- Add cornstarch, rice flour, coconut milk, sugar, salt, and 4 drops of purple colouring to the grated yam.
- Mix well, pour, and flatten into a greased 20 × 20 × 5 cm pan and steam for 25 minutes. Set aside.

Ingredients for Top Layer

100 ml coconut milk
350 ml water
15 g cornstarch
35 g rice flour
¼ tsp salt
1 tbsp sugar
3 pandan leaves

Method

- Mix the coconut milk with the water to get 450 ml of liquid.
- Mix the cornstarch and rice flour with some of the coconut-water liquid to form a smooth slurry.
- Mix the slurry into the coconut-water mixture and add salt and sugar.
- Cook the mixture together with the pandan leaves in a double boiler till thick, constantly stirring.

Finishing

- Pour the top layer over the yam base and steam over low to medium fire for another 20 minutes. Allow to cool when done, then only cut and serve when the cake has cooled down completely.

5. *Susi* Bun (Eurasian Savoury Meat Bun)

This savoury bun also known as *pang susi* originates from the Eurasian community in Malacca, often made during festive seasons. This version was one of Mama Chit's old recipes that deviates slightly from the norm; additional ingredients are added to the mince pork filling. One might say it has a Peranakan touch that hopefully would not rouse the ire of our Eurasian friends. The dough now uses a mixture of Japanese bread flour and Hong Kong flour, which Mum has developed over the years, that results in a soft, light, and moist bun. Simply delightful.

Makes about 24 buns

Ingredients for Buns

340 g Japanese bread flour
115 g Hong Kong flour
85 g icing sugar
115 g butter
1 tsp Bake King SP stabilizer
9 g dry yeast (Swallow brand)
60 ml water
½ tsp salt
*9 g bread improver**
3 tbsp condensed milk
1 egg
170 ml water
9 tsp milk powder

**RedMan brand from Phoon Huat is recommended.*

Method

- Mix the dry yeast with 60 ml water.
- Put everything into a mixing bowl and mix using a dough hook attachment, kneading till the dough is satiny in appearance.
- Proof the dough for 1 hour till it doubles in size.
- Scale into small balls, hand-knead, and shape individually using fingers and thumbs and sprinkling flour to prevent sticking.
- Line up the dough balls in a baking pan, then start inserting the filling.

Ingredients for Filling

340 g minced pork
1 tsp ketumbar *(coriander)*
2 tsp allspice powder
1 tbsp light soya sauce
1 tbsp of dark soya sauce
1 cube of chicken seasoning
½ tsp pepper
½ tsp salt
1 tbsp flour
2 tbsp Chinese wine
5 shallots, sliced
85 g tung kwa *(winter melon), chopped*
½ cup cilantro
1 potato, boiled and mashed

Method

- Fry the onions, then add the pork and *tung kwa.*
- Add in all the seasonings and continue frying, then add the flour slurry to thicken.
- Finally, add the mashed potato to give the filling some body.

Finishing

- Once all the balls have been filled and lined up nicely in a baking pan, proof the buns for another 35 minutes.
- Glaze the buns with an egg wash using an egg and cold liquid in a 1:1 ratio, meaning only one egg per tablespoon of cold liquid (water) blended with a whisk or fork. The best way to apply an egg wash to your pastry is with a pastry brush. A brush allows you to spread the wash in a nice thin layer over the pastry dough to add a nice colour and sheen to the buns.
- Bake the buns in an oven at 200°C for 5–8 minutes, then reduce the heat to 180°C for 10–12 minutes.

6. Mr Ma's Pudding

During her teaching days at Waterloo Girl's School, there was a gentleman in the school who was a janitor and handyman whose daily duties included refilling classroom blackboard chalk, duster, and inks for the teacher's pens – yes, this was a practice back then. Mum remembered him when she was a student at Raffles Girls' School, where he worked in a similar role. Interestingly, the kind-hearted principal who was supportive of him had one day organised a paid cooking class for the teachers so that Mr Ma could earn some extra money. Apparently, Mr Ma also possessed culinary skills and taught them a few recipes, one of which was a pudding which Mum found very tasty. It is a simple pudding recipe which she has since developed but continues to name it after Mr Ma.

Incidentally, there was another interesting story involving cooking from her time in this school. It involved one of Mum's students who came from a destitute family and whose father was unemployed. The same kind-hearted principal gave him an opportunity to start a food stall in the canteen and got Mum to spend a Saturday morning teaching him how to make mee *siam*. He learnt quickly, worked hard, and was successful in this endeavour. He was thereafter able to support his family. All one needs is an opportunity in life, and indeed, how very grateful he was to both ladies.

Ingredients for Pudding

4 egg whites
5 tbsp sugar
4 tsp gelatin
1 tbsp custard powder
180 g Nestlé cream
90 ml coconut milk
45 ml water
1 tsp vanilla essence

Ingredients for the Sauce

4 egg yolks
1 tbsp sugar
180 ml evaporated milk
1 tsp vanilla essence

Method

- Place the gelatin and custard powder in a saucepan; mix in the water to form a smooth paste.
- Add in the coconut milk and boil till thick, then set aside to cool.
- Whisk the egg whites with sugar till thick and frothy, then slowly mix it in with the coconut mixture. Add in the vanilla essence.
- Stir well, pour into moulds, and chill till it sets.
- Place all ingredients for the sauce into a double boiler or a saucepan over boiling water and stir till thick. Allow to chill.
- Serve the pudding with the sauce.

7. *Kueh Kodok* (Fried Banana Patties)

Pap and Mum used to frequent the senior police officers' mess at Mount Pleasant Road where at one time Pap was president of the mess committee. Back then, the mess had a Hainanese family who were live-in caterers/housekeepers for many years. Mrs Tan was an excellent cook, and she gave Mum this simple but delicious recipe and for some strange reason called it monkey cake. Great for when bananas get overripe, it is a common recipe, but Mrs Tan's had some little extras that made her *kueh kodok* that much better.

Ingredients

3 large bananas, sliced
2 eggs
3 tbsp evaporated milk
2 tbsp brown sugar
200 g flour
1 tsp baking powder
¼ tsp nutmeg powder
¼ tsp salt

Method

- Beat the eggs and sugar lightly.
- Mash the sliced bananas with a fork and add to the egg mixture together with the milk, nutmeg powder, salt, flour, and baking soda. Mix well.
- Use a spoon to scoop the batter; deep fry in hot oil till golden brown.

8. English Trifle

This is another of Mrs Tan's recipes. English trifle dates back to the Victorian era and is quite the opposite of what its name describes – trivial or of little importance. It is, in fact, far from that and is a rich and exquisite after-dinner dessert that uses a fair amount of alcohol – rum or sherry or even Drambuie liquor – or all the above? I guess it was appropriate that this dessert was then served in the senior police officer's mess that was and still is located in the same large old colonial bungalow. I believe their culinary traditions have evolved, and Mrs Tan has since passed on. Nevertheless, not only is this a great recipe but it also is another great leftover/repurposed recipe; Mrs Tan used leftover butter cake or sponge cake as the foundation for her trifle. Layered in a glass bowl with custard, fruits, or fruit cocktail and jello (gelatin dessert), it is colourful and presents beautifully. After cooling in the fridge to settle, it is topped with whipped cream and garnished with almonds and cherries. Wow, trust me, after this, it's back to the gym!

Ingredients

Leftover butter cake (preferred) or sponge cake (equivalent of 12 slices, 1 cm thick)
½ packet of strawberry or cherry jello
5 tbsp custard powder
180 ml evaporated milk
1 litre water
4 tbsp sugar
2 tbsp rum
1 large can of fruit cocktail
¼ tsp salt
20 g blanched sliced almonds
maraschino cherries
whipped cream

Method

- Completely dissolve ½ packet of strawberry jello in half cup of boiling water. When dissolved, add half a cup of water at room temperature. Set aside.
- To cook the custard, use a small amount of milk in the custard powder to form a slurry and slowly add the slurry to the boiling evaporated milk, water, sugar, and rum until it thickens.
- Using a large glass bowl to display the myriad of colours, line the bottom of the bowl with cake (first layer), scatter some fruit cocktail and almonds over the cake, and pour some jello and custard over the first layer. Repeat the process over three or four layers.
- Lastly, cover the uppermost layer of the trifle with whipped cream and garnish with cherries and almonds.
- Chill in the fridge to allow the jello to set, then serve.

9. Mum's Mulligatawny Soup

This is another colonial recipe that has a myriad of variations but is essentially a spicy or curry-flavoured soup. Historically, this dish goes back a couple of centuries during the days of the British Raj; and in Tamil, it means pepper water. This is a good example of fusion food (Anglo-Indian), and the reason for its existence in its present form was the fussy British colonists and soldiers refusing to alter their way of dining; a soup course must be included in the meal. Not having an equivalent soup dish and rather than serving the popular local pepper water, the servants mellowed the spiciness, included some meat and vegetables, and thickened the soup, making it more palatable for their colonial masters. It became so popular that it made its way back to Britain. In Singapore, you can find this dish in some Indian restaurants, but it is still popular on the menus at the Singapore Cricket Club, Tanglin Club, and Raffles Hotel, bastions of a bygone colonial era. Having served in the police force through the colonial era, Pap enjoyed the soup and got Mum to perfect it to his taste. Combining recipes that she found including the one served at the senior police officer's mess, she came up with this version.

Ingredients A

1 chicken or 800 g chicken parts
3 tbsp ketumbar *(coriander) powder*
½ tsp cinnamon powder
1 tbsp jintan puteh *(cumin) powder*
1 tsp nutmeg powder
1 tbsp jintan manis *(fennel) powder*
½ tsp clove powder
1 tsp turmeric powder
½ tsp star anise powder
1 tbsp chilli powder
1 tsp black pepper

Ingredients B

200 ml coconut milk
45 g garlic paste
85 g onions, sliced
85 g onion paste
2 sprigs of curry leaves
60 ml lime juice
¼ tsp salt
1 tbsp tamarind water from 1 seed

Garnish

shredded chicken
½ cup fried shallots
½ cup cilantro, chopped

Method

- Boil the chicken in water to get 1.5 litres of stock. Shred the chicken and set aside the stock.
- Mix ingredients A together and, with some water, form a paste.
- Fry the sliced onions till slightly brown, then add the onion and garlic paste.

- Add in the mulligatawny powder paste and the curry leaves; fry till fragrant.
- Add the chicken stock, lime juice, coconut milk, salt, and tamarind water.
- Boil till ready to serve, garnished with shredded chicken, fried shallots, and cilantro.

Note: The soup can be served in several ways – with some cooked rice added into it, with bread, or with *putu mayam*. Add some sambal *belachan* into the soup for a touch of Peranakan fusion.

10. Oxtail Stew

This oxtail stew recipe is yet another one of those obtained from an unlikely source and strangely enough from a vegetable vendor at Tekka Market in Little India! During her working years, Mum often did her grocery shopping at Tekka Market, and on one trip, the vegetable vendor was boasting to her that he used to be a chef at the Marco Polo Hotel. The award-winning Marco Polo Hotel was one of Singapore's famous landmarks. Many popular personalities, including movie stars and politicians, chose to stay there in the 1970s and 1980s. The restaurants and coffee house there were also very popular. The hotel was torn down in 1999, and on its site now sits a condominium. Anyway, the vegetable vendor was bragging that his oxtail stew was the best in Singapore. That, of course, got Mum going, and he promised to give her the recipe the next time she visited. Normally, she took between ten days and two weeks to do her shopping there, but she appeared again two days later to see if he was sincere. Not only was he sincere but he also lent her his personal handwritten recipe book, which she made a copy of and returned to him a week later. I guess he wasn't joking when he said his was the best; I would admit that it is very good, excellent when served over a bed of mashed potatoes or eaten with French loaf. Bon appétit!

Ingredients A

4 kg oxtail – serves 12 pax
30 g cake flour
1 tsp paprika
1 tbsp olive oil
1 tsp black pepper
2 bay leaves
½ tsp rosemary
¼ tsp thyme
1 litre packet of Campbell's beef stock
1 can of beer or stout or a glass of red
1 tbsp of Bisto gravy mixed with some wine water

Ingredients B

7 big white onions, chopped
700 g carrots, chopped
170 g celery, cut 5 cm in length
700 g potatoes, cubed
1 can of button mushrooms
3 strips of bacon, cut in half
1 tin of baked beans
1 small can of tomato puree
¼ tsp salt
1 sweet potato, boiled and mashed

Method

- Remove fat from the oxtail, wash, and dry the meat.
- Smear olive oil all over the meat. Put the cake flour, paprika, and black pepper into a large ziplock bag and swirl the meat in the bag till coated.
- Line up the meat in a baking tray and bake in the oven at 180°C until the meat is browned and fragrant. Set aside.

- Chop 3 large onions, 250 g carrots, and 170 g celery and place into the bottom of the stovetop pressure cooker.
- Add the baked oxtail over the vegetables in the pressure cooker, together with bay leaves, thyme, and rosemary. Add half a cup of water and pressure-cook at high heat until the gauge button pops up. Then turn down the heat to low for 18 minutes for fresh oxtail or 25 minutes for frozen oxtail. Once completed, carefully depressurise the cooker, remove the meat, and set aside.
- Meanwhile, cut the potatoes into cubes, 450 g carrots in wedges, and cut into halves the 3 big onions and slice the fourth. Set aside.
- Fry the bacon, then add in the sliced onion and caramelise with 1 tsp sugar till brown.
- Place the caramelised bacon and onions into a cooking pot, then add in the cut potatoes, carrots, and onions; beef stock; stout (or beer or wine); and Bisto gravy mix.
- Add in the oxtail and bring to a boil.
- Stir well, then add the baked beans and tomato puree.
- To thicken the stew, puree the vegetables from the pressure cooker together with the mashed sweet potato and add to the stew.
- Add salt and sugar to taste, if required.

Note: When the stew is ready, serve over a bed of mashed potatoes or with French loaf.

11. Mee *Siam* (Siamese Noodles)

Mee *siam* had its roots in northern Malaysia (Penang) with Siamese (Thai) influence. It is a very popular comfort food for many Singaporeans; hence, there exist countless recipes for this dish. Mum typically collected recipes from any source, and if she assessed the recipe to be good (I suppose by experience and studying the ingredients in the recipe and how the dish is prepared) and if they intrigued her, she would try them, then worked on perfecting them. One such recipe that didn't need much refinement, though, was the mee *siam* recipe given to Mum by her old friend, the late Mrs Shirley Oh. Mum had previously tried many mee *siam* recipes but, in her opinion, found this one to be the best – just the right combination and amounts of *taucheo*, *assam*, and sugar as well as *belachan*, which is not often used in mee *siam*. This recipe also includes ground nuts similar in style to the Indian variety. Shirley was also married to a police officer, and interestingly, at home, we would always refer to this dish as Shirley Oh's mee *siam*. I think it pays a nice tribute to Shirley, and she is always fondly remembered when Mum serves mee *siam*.

Ingredients for *Bee Hoon*

- 600 bee hoon, *soaked and dried*
- *300 g* taugeh *(bean sprouts)*
- *500 g prawns, deshelled, shells saved for prawn stock*
- *4 cloves of garlic*
- *3 tsp dried chilli paste*
- *2 tbsp sugar*
- *1 tsp salt*
- *1 large white onion, sliced*
- *1 tbsp dried prawns, soaked*
- *½ cup oil*

Method

- Deshell the prawns and rub in salt, sugar, and baking soda for 10 minutes, then wash and dry the prawns.
- Fry the shells lightly, then add water to make 2 litres of prawn stock. Set aside.
- Grind into a paste the garlic, chilli paste, sugar, and salt.
- Fry the ground ingredients till fragrant and set aside.
- Use 2 tsp of the fried ingredients, and fry the 500 g prawns. When cooked, slice in halves and set aside for garnishing.
- Fry the sliced onion in half a cup of oil till slightly brown.
- Add in the fried ingredients and 1 tbsp of dried prawns.
- Finally, add in the *bee hoon* and *taugeh*. Fry evenly till cooked, resulting in a reddish-orange tinge to the *bee hoon*. Set aside.

Ingredients for Gravy

- *3 tsp dried chilli paste*
- *3 cloves of garlic*
- *2 large white onions*
- *2.5 cm cube of* belachan
- *3 tbsp brown* taucheo
- *½ cup brown peanuts*

½ cup ground cashew nuts

6 candlenuts, roasted

Additional Ingredients

3 tbsp oil

3 tbsp sugar

2 litres prawn stock

200 ml coconut milk (optional)

120 g assam*, mixed with 250 ml water, removing the seeds*

Method

- Grind ingredients B into a paste.
- Heat 3 tbsp oil and fry ingredients B till oil breaks.
- Add in 2 litres prawn stock, assam water, and 3 tbsp sugar.
- To enrich the gravy, add 200 ml coconut milk (optional).
- Bring to a boil and add salt and sugar to taste, if required.

Garnish

500 g fried prawns, sliced in half

6 boiled eggs, sliced in quarters

2 tau kwa*, cut in small cubes and fried*

6 calamansi, cut in halves

½ cup ku chai *(garlic chives), chopped*

Finishing

- Serve the mee *siam* in a deep plate.
- Place some *bee hoon* in the plate and garnish with prawns, boiled eggs, *tau kwa*, *ku chai*, and half a calamansi to give the dish a sourish kick, if fancied.
- Generously pour gravy over the noodles and add a blob of sambal *tumis*.

12. *Hong Siew* Fish Head (Braised Fish Head)

Back in the '70s, Pap would often bring the family to this simple Cantonese-style family eatery at Tan Quee Lan Street. It was known as Tai Sun Restaurant (not to be confused with other similarly named businesses) and was located among a run-down row of shophouses. The building is now a refurbished heritage site that today houses apartments and many stylish restaurants. His favourite dish there was the *hong siew* fish head which, in his opinion, was the best he had tasted. Of course, Mum was forever chasing after the recipe quite unsuccessfully, until the day the owners decided to close down the restaurant. Mum then told the proprietress that Pap would not get to eat his favourite dish again after they ceased operations. So Mum persuaded her to share the recipe. The lady, being empathetic to a regular customer, gave in. This recipe is excellent. When a sizeable fish head or fish is cooked with all the ingredients added, this becomes a balanced one-dish meal of fish, meat, and vegetables and, when eaten with white rice, will feed a family of eight or ten.

Ingredients A

800 g fish head (red snapper or grouper), chopped into large chunks, or a whole fish (preferably small grouper or threadfin, 800 g–1 kg)
1 egg white
2 tbsp cornflour
½ tsp garlic paste
1 big onion, sliced
2 small carrots, cut into chunks
½ wong ah pak *(Chinese/napa cabbage)*
6 dried shiitake mushrooms, soaked till soft and sliced
400 g siew yoke *(roasted pork belly)*
1 small can of button mushrooms
½ winter melon, cut into cubes
2 packets of egg tofu, sliced into coins (2½ cm thick) and fried

Ingredients B

1½ tbsp oyster sauce
3 tsp sesame oil
1 tbsp light soya sauce
2 tbsp Chinese wine (Hua Tiao Chiew)
2 tsp sugar
½ tsp dark soya sauce
2 cups chicken stock

Method

- Pat the fish dry and marinate with egg white and some salt, then cover it completely using a small sift with cornflour. (Tapioca or potato flour can also be used.)
- Shallow-fry the fish in heated oil and set aside.
- Fry the garlic paste and sliced onion, then add in the *siew yoke*, carrots, and soaked shiitake mushrooms.
- Add in ingredients B, followed by sliced *wong ah pak*, winter melon, and button mushrooms. Cover and simmer for 10 minutes.

- Thicken with a cornflour slurry.
- Place the fish in the centre of the wok and continue simmering with the vegetables for another 5 minutes.
- Beat an egg and stir into the dish till cooked.
- Finally, add in the egg tofu and garnish with cilantro and slices of chilli.

13. Katong White *Bee Hoon* (Fried Rice Vermicelli)

This fried *bee hoon* dish is better known to the family as Annie's white *bee hoon*. Why Annie called it *katong* white *bee hoon* I don't really know. Annie was Pap's personal assistant/secretary, a lively Peranakan lady who has since passed on. It was at an office potluck occasion when Mum laid eyes on a large Tupperware container filled with delectable white *bee hoon*. Upon tasting it, Mum was impressed and immediately sought to obtain the recipe. She found out that Annie had brought it and, of course, wanted to know how the *bee hoon* remained in strands rather than breaking up, which often happens in the cooking process, and what made it so tasty. Annie was eventually persuaded to share the recipe, which she swore was her great-grandmother's secret *bee hoon* recipe. I guess it's no longer a secret, and by the way, it is really good.

Ingredients A

1 packet (400 g) white bee hoon *(Tai Shan Saga Chilli brand recommended)*
½ kg taugeh *(bean sprouts), soaked in sugar water to remain crunchy and drained when ready to cook*
3 pieces of large fried fish cake, sliced thinly
1 piece of belly pork, boiled and sliced thinly
170 g prawns, deshelled and sliced thinly
1 squid, sliced thinly
2 tbsp garlic paste
½ tbsp salt
1 cube of chicken seasoning
1 tbsp sugar
1½ tbsp fish sauce
½ cup chopped cilantro
½ cup oil
4 tbsp butter

Garnish

½ cup fried shallots
2 fresh red chillies, seeds removed and sliced finely lengthwise
½ cup shredded cucumber
2 eggs, fried in an omelette and sliced finely
sambal belachan

Method

- Boil the prawn shells and belly pork in water to get 500 ml stock. Remove the belly pork and shells, strain, and set stock aside.
- Slice the prawn meat into little cubes and slice the fish cake, boiled belly pork, and squid thinly.
- Using 120 ml oil, fry the garlic paste and the shredded ingredients till cooked, then pour all the fried ingredients into the stock.
- Add into the stock the sugar, fish sauce, salt, and chicken cube. (Stock should be a little sweeter and saltish than usual as this will go into the *bee hoon* and *taugeh*.)

- Using 2 tbsp butter and ½ cup oil, fry the *bee hoon* and *taugeh*.
- Add in the stock and ingredients a ladle at a time to moisten and fry the *bee hoon* evenly.
- When cooked, add the chopped cilantro and 2 tbsp butter to enhance the flavour and add a sheen to the *bee hoon*.
- Garnish with fried shallots, sliced omelette, sliced red chillies, and shredded cucumber.
- Sambal *belachan* goes great with the dish.

Note: To maintain the springiness of the *bee hoon* and prevent it from breaking when frying:

1. Boil water with a little oil and salt.
2. Blanch the dry *bee hoon*, stir, and let it boil for one minute only.
3. Transfer the *bee hoon* into another container and cover it for 5 minutes.
4. It will be 80 per cent cooked and ready for frying – do not fry for too long.

14. Mee *Rebus* (Boiled Noodles)

Mum learnt this recipe from a Malay *mak cik* (auntie) who was a school hawker at Toa Payoh School when Mum was teaching there. All her teacher friends at school laughed at her for thinking that the mee *rebus* was good. After all, it just cost twenty cents at the time. What Mum recognised in the school hawker's mee *rebus* was the taste and substance of the dish. She also recognised that due to the low price and the cost of preparation, it would naturally be diluted. Upon learning the recipe, she enhanced it with more spices and ingredients and – voila! – an excellent mee *rebus* with a nice thick gravy accompanied with garnishing such as boiled egg, fried tofu, green chilli, cilantro leaves, fried shallots, and a dollop of sambal *tumis*. I like mine with a *bergedil* (potato cutlet).

Ingredients A

2.5 cm piece of ginger
2 cloves of garlic
8 shallots
4 cm piece of lengkuas *(blue ginger)*
1 tsp dried chilli paste
1 tsp kunyit *(turmeric) powder*
1 cm cube of belachan
3 buah keras *(candlenut)*

Ingredients B

1 kg yellow noodles (mee), scalded (serves 10 pax)
½ kg taugeh *(bean sprouts), soaked in sugar water to remain crunchy and drained when ready to scald*
2 tsp ketumbar *(coriander) powder*
1 tsp jintan puteh *(cumin) powder*
4 stalks of serai *(lemongrass), bruised*
150 g ground roasted peanuts
100 g dried prawns, soaked and pounded
2 tbsp taucheo
2 orange sweet potatoes, boiled and mashed
3 dried whole cuttlefish
30 g ikan bilis *(dried anchovies), pounded*
1 tomato, sliced in half
sugar and salt to taste
1 litre Campbell's beef stock
1 litre water
2 tbsp cake flour mixed with some water to form a slurry

Garnish

½ cup cilantro, chopped
15 green chillies, sliced
10 calamansi, cut in half
½ cup spring onions, chopped
8 boiled eggs, cut into quarters
2 firm tofu, deep-fried sliced
½ cup fried shallots
sambal tumis

Method

- Grind ingredients A into a fine paste.
- Mix the *ketumbar* and *jintan puteh* into the ground ingredients.
- Fry the mixed ingredients in 3 tbsp oil till the oil breaks.
- Add in the bruised *serai*, pounded dried prawns, ground roasted peanuts, and *taucheo*. Continue frying, then add in the dried cuttlefish, pounded *ikan bilis*, and tomato.
- Add 1 litre beef stock and 1 litre water and bring to a boil.
- Finally, add in the mashed sweet potato and slurry to thicken the gravy.
- Add sugar and salt to taste.

Finishing

- Place the noodles and *taugeh* in a deep plate and pour gravy over generously.
- Garnish with sliced egg, fried tofu, cilantro, green chilli, spring onions, fried shallots, and calamansi.
- Finally, add a few drops of dark soya sauce and a dollop of sambal *tumis*.

15. Lontong Sayur Lodeh (Vegetables in Coconut Milk)

It is strange I know, but it seems Mum learnt several recipes from the school hawkers where she taught. As far as she was concerned, she didn't discriminate on where the recipes came from; she was more interested in how they tasted. In time, testing these against other similar recipes from other sources, she maintains that the ones given her in these most unlikely places still win the taste test. This recipe came from the same *mak cik* in Toa Payoh School, who was always friendly and willing to teach the teacher. I suppose the connection through language, as Mum speaks Malay fluently, always helped. Through the years, the original recipe has been enhanced to include more ingredients that has perfected the taste and quality of the dish. This dish is commonly called *lontong* in Singapore when, in fact, *lontong* is compressed rice cakes usually wrapped in banana leaves that is served with *sayur lodeh*. *Sayur lodeh* is essentially a yellowish-coloured broth comprising vegetables cooked till soft in coconut milk accompanied with *tau kwa*, hard boiled eggs, and tempeh. It is served with *serunding kelapa* and sambal *tumis*. I would add a *bergedil* and some rendang to the dish to make it a full, flavourful, and satisfying meal.

Recipe serves 10 pax

Ingredients A

3 buah keras *(candlenut)*
4 cloves of garlic
6 shallots
4 cm piece of lengkuas *(blue ginger)*
1 tbsp dried chilli paste
2 cm piece of kunyit *(turmeric)*
1 cm cube of belachan
2 tbsp of ground roasted peanuts
2 stalks of serai *(lemongrass)*

Ingredients B

30 g dried prawns, soaked and pounded
1 tsp jeera (roasted cumin) powder
½ tbsp ketumbar *(coriander) powder*
2 fresh green chillies
4 daun salam *(local bay leaves)*
1 daun limau perut *(kaffir lime leaf)*

Ingredients C

60 ml evaporated milk
500 ml coconut milk
1.5 litre water
1 cube of fish seasoning
½ tsp salt
230 g long beans, cut 5 cm in length
300 g white cabbage, sliced
2 carrots, cut into sticks
2 christophine (chayote), cut in cubes
2 firm tofu, cut in 8 triangles and fried

1 packet lontong *rice, steamed before use*
serunding kelapa
sambal tumis

Method

- Fry the tofu and set aside.
- Grind ingredients A into a fine paste and fry in 3 tbsp oil till the oil breaks.
- Add in the dried prawns, jeera, and *ketumbar*, followed by the green chilli, *daun salam*, and *daun limau perut.*
- When fragrant, add in the premixed coconut milk and water and the evaporated milk, together with the fish cube and salt. Bring to a boil.
- Finally, add in the vegetables and fried tofu.

Finishing

- Place some *lontong* rice in a deep plate and generously pour over the vegetables and gravy.
- Garnish with *serunding kelapa* and a dollop of sambal *tumis.*

16. Mum's Chicken *Musallam*

Shortly after Pap had left immigration in late 1974, he was invited by Singapore Airlines (SIA) on an inaugural flight to Amsterdam – of course, with the wife. Mum was very excited as this was her first trip to Europe and flying first class. She found the meals very palatable, but one dish in particular intrigued her. It was called chicken *musallam* and was probably some variation of murgh *musallam*, which is a Mughlai whole chicken dish marinated in a variety of spices. Whatever the case, she liked the SIA variation and obviously was not able to acquire the recipe. She found that the dish reminded her a little of Mama Chit's *ayam sio* with significant addition of Indian spices. So using that as her premise, she experimented and produced what we now call Mum's chicken *musallam*, which Pap declared tasted the same as the SIA dish.

Ingredients A

800 g chicken, cut in pieces
225 g shallot paste
3 tbsp sugar
½ tbsp tamarind

Ingredients B

5 tbsp coriander powder
1 tsp turmeric powder
½ tsp black pepper
2 tsp cumin powder
2 tsp fennel powder

Ingredients C

1 large white onion, sliced
3 stalks of lemongrass, bruised
2 fresh green chillies
120 ml evaporated milk
120 ml chicken stock

Method

- Marinate the chicken with the rest of ingredients A. Set aside.
- Add some water to ingredients B to make a paste.
- Fry the sliced onion with 3 tbsp of oil, then add the paste and fry till fragrant.
- Add in the chicken, lemongrass, and whole green chillies.
- Finally, add in the milk and chicken stock and salt to taste.
- Boil till chicken is tender and gravy is rich and thick.
- Serve with rice.

17. Mutton Keema

Jaswant Singh was somewhat of an all-round handyman. Professionally, he was a driving instructor and somehow had a lot of schoolteachers as his students. Mum learnt driving from him, and he also provided transport services (more like pirate taxi services) to teachers to and from school. Funnily enough, Pap also knew him. In one of our travel adventures when we were kids, Pap had engaged him to drive the family all the way to Penang in his old Mercedes-Benz. He really enjoyed driving and drove fast. Anyway, Mr Singh, as I used to address him, gave Mum this mutton keema recipe that he swore by; and naturally, it is served with chapati. He told Mum he enjoyed this more than driving, and having eaten it on many an occasion, I understand why he said that.

Ingredients A

5 cloves of garlic
10 shallots
1½ cm ginger
3 fresh green chillies, seeds removed
¼ cup spring onions
½ cup cilantro, chopped

Ingredients B

2 tbsp of garam masala
2 tsp turmeric powder
2 tsp chilli powder

Ingredients C

500 g minced mutton
1 carrot, diced
2 potatoes, diced
1 cup green peas

Method

- Add some water to ingredients B to make a paste.
- Grind ingredients A into a fine paste. Using 3 tbsp oil, fry the ground ingredients.
- Add in the paste from Ingredients B and fry till fragrant.
- Add in the minced mutton and continue to fry over low fire.
- Finally, add in the diced carrots, potatoes, and green peas.
- When ready, serve with chapati.

18. Black Mutton

When Pap was controller of immigration, he noticed that one of his senior officers was always eating in and hardly ever went out to lunch. He also noticed that he ate practically the same thing every day, a dark-coloured meat, alternating the carbo supplement between roti and basmati rice. Not able to keep his curiosity in check, he asked him one day what he was eating. The officer, who was of Pakistani descent, offered him a small piece to try. Pap was so impressed that he asked him if he could have another small piece to take home for Mum to try. Upon tasting it, it became an obsession for Mum to get the recipe to try cooking it herself. Finally, at an office event one day, she met with the officer's wife and boldly asked her for the recipe. His wife was a little reluctant to share it initially, but I guess when the wife of her husband's boss asked, she folded and parted with the recipe. We call it black mutton, and I'm sure there's probably a proper name for it, but Mum never asked. It is a lovely, spicy, and delectable dish that makes one want to eat it every day.

Ingredients A

25 pieces of mutton chops (preferably bone-in lamb ribs)
1 tsp garlic paste
1 tsp ginger paste
½ tsp salt
1 tbsp black pepper

Ingredients B

1 stick of cinnamon, 5 cm long
5 cloves
5 cardamom seeds

Ingredients C

1 tsp jeera (roasted cumin) powder
½ tbsp of fennel powder

Ingredients D

8 large white onions, chopped finely
8 tomatoes, chopped finely

Method

- Marinate the meat with the rest of ingredients A for 1 hour.
- Using 5 tbsp oil, fry the ingredients B.
- Add in the chopped onions and fry till all are coated with oil.
- Add in the chopped tomatoes and fry till well mixed.
- Add in the ingredients C, then the marinated mutton chops. Fry initially on high heat, then cover the pot and lower the fire to medium to simmer. Do not add water; the meat must be cooked in the onions and tomatoes.
- When the mutton is cooked (about an hour) and the gravy is thick, remove the chops, set aside the gravy, and line the meat in a baking tray.
- Bake in the oven at 200°C till the meat is brownish-black, then turn over.
- When completed, replace the gravy on the meat and serve.

19. Sarawak Prawns

In the latter years of his career, one of Pap's duties as a deputy commissioner was to build and foster relationships for better cooperation and collaboration with the police forces of the countries around the region. Like all regional meetings, there would be an agenda for discussion, but the real relationship building came after the meetings over dinner and drinks. Mum accompanied him to many of these meetings, and typically, the wives would be looked after by their counterparts to lunch, shop, or visit cultural sites during the day. At one of these meetings in Kuching, Sarawak, she was brought to a simple but excellent eatery in Downtown Kuching. There, she sampled a prawn dish that intrigued her. A young, 17-year-old boy lingering around the table proudly told her that he cooked it. When she asked how, he invited her into the kitchen and shared that he used real salted egg in the dish. Interestingly, this was before salted egg as an ingredient became a craze in Singapore. Today this ingredient is commonly used for many dishes and comes packaged in powdered form. Mum calls this dish Sarawak prawns.

Ingredients A

500 g medium to large prawns, heads removed and butterflied, leaving the tails intact
1 fresh red chilli, chopped
1 sprig of curry leaves
2 salted egg yolks
½ tsp garlic paste
3 tbsp evaporated milk
½ tsp sugar
2 tbsp butter

Method

- Deep fry the prawns quickly in oil. Remove and set aside
- Using 2 tbsp butter, fry the garlic paste, then red chilli, salted egg yolks, and curry leaves till fragrant.
- Add in prawns with the evaporated milk and sugar.
- Stir-fry, and when ready to serve, garnish with fried shallots.

20. Langkawi Fish

At another regional meeting, this time in Penang, the Malaysian hosts organised a one-day yacht cruise after the meetings from Penang to Langkawi and back. Apparently, it turned out to be a minor disaster as the waters were rough, and almost all were seasick. Funnily enough, Mum was not affected – perhaps her sea legs were holding up. Not wanting to be with all the green-faced passengers, she went down to the small galley where the chef was preparing a fish dish. He didn't mind her standing beside him as he cooked lunch, and she, needless to say, took notes. Mum calls this dish Langkawi fish. It is cooked Malay-style; the whole fish is initially fried with spices, then topped with *rempah* using a variety of other spices and a sweet and sour sauce. Anyone who loves eating fish will absolutely savour this one.

Ingredients A

6 pieces or 500 g angkoli *(sea bream) steaks*
1 tsp jintan manis *(fennel) powder*
1 tsp kunyit *(turmeric) powder*
1 tsp chilli powder
½ tsp fish powder

Ingredients B

10 cloves of garlic
140 g shallots
2.5 cm piece of ginger

Ingredients C

2 large onions, sliced
6 cardamoms
1 cinnamon bark (5 cm long)
6 cloves
1 tsp chilli powder
1 tsp jeera (roasted cumin) powder
½ tsp jintan puteh *(cumin) powder*
1 tbsp tomato ketchup
1 tsp vinegar
1 tsp dark soya sauce

Method

- Marinate the fish with the rest of ingredients A and set aside for half an hour.
- Fry the fish in shallow oil till cooked, then set aside.
- Grind ingredients B into a fine paste.
- Fry the onions in 3 tbsp oil, then add in the paste.
- Continue frying, then add in the remainder of the ingredients C, including the sauces.
- Season with salt and sugar to taste.
- Finally, add in the fish and stir-fry to coat the fish with the thick *rempah*.

SUCCESS AND ABUNDANCE

Both my parents retired from the civil service in 1984. Pap had a successful career in the police force and rose to the highest rank he could attain as a non-university graduate, and Mum was only too pleased to have more time on her hands to cook at leisure instead of baking to supplement their income. I guess they must have planned the timing of their respective retirements and were looking forward to receiving their pensions, which were still relevant in their day. For many years now, there is no longer a national government pension scheme in Singapore; and instead, the Central Provident Fund (CPF) scheme is administered for all. Their timing for retirement could not have been better as, by then, my sister and I completed our overseas tertiary education, and my brother was already established as a pilot in the air force. They no longer needed to support us, and Pap was appointed the executive director of the Singapore Manufacturers' Association. So with a salary, a pension, and no children to support, for the first time in their lives, they didn't have to scrimp and count their pennies.

They were now able to fulfil their dreams of travelling the world as both enjoyed experiencing different cultures, sights, and foods. Their first big trip, immediately upon retirement, took them through the United States, Canada, and Europe on a round-the-world ticket, a retirement gift from the police force. My sister, my fiancée (now my wife), and I joined them for the European leg, rented a car in London, and drove across Europe. What an adventure navigating by paper maps that were not entirely accurate; there was no such thing then as Google Maps, mobile phones, or the internet. This was back in 1984, and we did it on our own, including searching for hotels or a bed and breakfast along the way. What a difference technology makes. I can't even imagine making a trip today without the aid of technology.

Anyway, whilst in Amsterdam, there was an interesting incident while we were walking around. Pap had disappeared, and from a distance, we saw him confronted by three Chinese men. When he rejoined us, he explained that the three men were former Singapore secret society members who had fled the country in the 1970s. They asked if he was there to arrest them as they were probably on the wanted list back home. Laughingly, he told them he was retired and there on holiday and wished them well. It seemed they were members of an established international triad organisation that were successful in their underground endeavours across Europe.

Just before starting his new job at SMA, the folks spent three months travelling across India and Sri Lanka, thoroughly enjoying the culture, culinary experience, and sightseeing. Pap always had a fascination with history, and for him, India has such a deep, rich, and varied history and culture that required the three-month investment in time. Of course, the cuisine also varied across the vast country. We share some of the recipes from that trip. Subsequent trips to Central America, the United States, the Caribbean, Middle East, North Africa, northern Europe, Australia, New Zealand, and neighbouring Asian countries checked off most of their travel bucket list, which also included several pilgrimages.

Around this time, the grandchildren were also growing up, and they did spend much time with them in between travels. Grandpa was always the storyteller, and Grandma would feed them. Family holidays were eventful and never dull and always with good food. Later in life when walking was no longer easy and Pap was wheelchair bound, they enjoyed going on cruises. All in all, I would say they made up for all the hard work during their careers and thoroughly enjoyed themselves in the twenty-plus years of retirement before Pap passed away in 2007. They lived well and ate well.

1. Kashmiri Chicken

On their three-month trip across India and Sri Lanka, Pap and Mum spent a few days in the mountainous and troubled but beautiful region of Kashmir. They stayed in a houseboat on Dal Lake and went back and forth to land via shikaras. They enjoyed their meals served on the veranda of the houseboat. One dish that stood out was Kashmiri chicken served with Kashmiri pilau. It was tender, succulent, and tasty. Mum charmingly complimented the chef, who was only too pleased to teach her how to cook the dish.

Ingredients

700 g chicken, cut into bite sizes
5 large onions, sliced thinly
1 tbsp garlic paste
1 tbsp ginger paste
2 tsp curry powder
4 tomatoes, sliced
½ tsp sugar
½ tsp light soya sauce
½ tsp salt
½ tsp black pepper
a pinch of saffron in a little hot water

Method

- Fry in 3 tbsp oil 2 large thinly sliced onions, tomatoes, garlic, and ginger paste till fragrant.
- Add in the remaining large onions and chicken pieces.
- Fry the chicken, adding the curry powder, salt, sugar, soya sauce, pepper, and saffron water.
- Cover and cook till the chicken is tender for about 20–30 minutes.
- When cooked, remove the chicken and puree the gravy.
- Recombine the chicken and gravy and set to boil evenly.
- Serve with Kashmiri pilau.

2. Kashmiri Pilau (Kashmiri Rice Dish)

Since the chicken was served with pilau, we complete the set with the Kashmiri pilau recipe. The chef on the houseboat was generous to provide both. Most variations of Kashmiri pilau will use a mix of dry fruits and nuts, but the foundation is most certainly basmati rice and saffron. Some even add fresh fruits, entirely customisable depending on your preferences. It is quite versatile as this aromatic rice dish can be served with other curries, meat, or vegetable dishes. A little trick to make it look grand, as if served in a maharaja's palace, is to use a little edible silver paper sprinkled on top (can be purchased in Little India).

Ingredients A

1.2 kg basmati rice (serves 15–18 pax)
5 tbsp ghee
6 shallots, ground
1 tsp garlic paste
½ tsp ginger paste
1.25 litres chicken stock
280 ml low-fat milk
15 almonds, blanched and ground
1½ tsp salt
¼ tsp rose essence
pinch of saffron in a little hot water
1 tbsp vegetable oil
2 bay leaves
½ cup cilantro
½ cup mint leaves

Ingredients B

1 stick of cinnamon bark (5 cm long)
6 cardamoms
6 cloves

Garnish

1 tsp mace
2 tbsp fried shallots
1 small box of raisins, fried in butter
pinch of grated carrots for colour
½ cup pistachios or almonds or cashew nuts

Method

- Soak the rice for one hour and drain.
- Fry ingredients B in ghee and 1 tbsp vegetable oil, then add in the ground shallots, ginger, and garlic paste and fry till fragrant.
- Add in the rice and fry evenly, then add in the chicken stock, milk, ground almond paste, and salt.
- Add in the bay leaves, rose essence, and saffron water before covering to cook the rice.
- When the rice is cooked, discard the spices and bay leaves and stir in the cilantro and mint.
- Cook for a few minutes more, then rake the rice and serve on a large serving dish complete with the garnishing on top.

3. Mutton Mysore

From the northernmost region of Kashmir to the southern part of India, the city of Mysore (or Mysuru) is rich in cultural heritage and majestic monuments, boasting magnificent palaces and heritage structures. From a culinary perspective and street food, they are famous for their idli, vada (*vadai* in Singapore), dosa (*thosai*), uttapam, and *theses*, to name a few more familiar foods amongst a myriad of delightful foods that are found there, including biryanis and scrumptious rice dishes, chutneys, curries, and desserts. Having gone into a restaurant one day, Pap ordered a sumptuous lunch that included mutton Mysore. Being the only Chinese/non-Indian in the restaurant and with Mum raving over the mutton Mysore, the staff there were tickled over how appreciative the foreigners were of their food. Mum immediately went into action, and before long, the chef shared his recipes. In fact, this mutton Mysore recipe is almost identical to the dish that was served at the century-old Islamic restaurant in the old days.

Ingredients A

1 kg mutton, cut in medium-sized cubes
1 large onion, chopped
6 shallots, sliced
1 tbsp garlic paste
1 tsp ginger paste
½ cup cilantro
½ cup spring onions

Ingredients B

1 tbsp ketumbar *(coriander) powder*
1 tsp fennel seeds powder
2 tsp jeera (roasted cumin) powder
½ tbsp black pepper

Method

- Fry ingredients A except the mutton in 3 tbsp oil.
- Add some water to ingredients B to make a paste and add/fry with fried ingredients A.
- Add in the mutton and either pressure-cook for 10 minutes or cook in the Crockpot for 2 hours till mutton is tender and the gravy thick and oily.
- Season with salt and sugar to taste and serve.

4. Mango Chutney

At the same restaurant, they served an excellent mango chutney appetiser that came with the meal. Mum continues to use this recipe today even if she has tried others. It comes with the perfect balance of tanginess and sweet and sour piquancy that makes it a brilliant accompaniment to spicy dishes.

Ingredients

6 green mangoes
2 cloves of garlic, sliced
7 g fresh ginger, sliced
55 g preserved ginger, sliced
12 almonds, blanched and sliced
2 tsp raisins
2 tbsp dried chilli paste
120 ml white vinegar
180 g sugar
1½ tsp salt

Method

- Peel and finely slice the mangoes.
- Boil the vinegar, sugar, and salt till it starts to thicken.
- Add the chilli paste, garlic, and ginger and stir well.
- After 10 minutes, add in the mango slices and boil till transparent.
- Add in the raisins and almonds while boiling, being careful not to overboil if mangoes are to remain in slices.
- Remove and cool.

5. Fried Bhindi Masala (Fried Okra Masala)

At another restaurant in Mysore, they ordered a delectable fried okra masala dish. Interestingly, the name *okra* comes from Nigeria, from the Igbo language. The plant apparently originated in Ethiopia, Africa, and arrived in South Asia via the Middle East, although there is still much dispute over this. Bhindi masala is a healthy dish made with okra, whole and ground spices, and onions in a semi-dry curry that goes very well as a side with rice or roti. Some northern Indian recipes use tomatoes.

Ingredients A

15 pieces of okra, sliced, 1 cm thick
1 tbsp panch phoron *(Indian five-spice)*
1 sprig of curry leaves
1 fresh green chilli, sliced
3 shallots, sliced
3 cloves of garlic, sliced

Ingredients B

1 large onion, sliced
¼ tsp grated ginger
½ tbsp garam masala
½ tsp chilli powder
½ tsp jeera (roasted cumin) powder
½ tsp sambar powder
¼ tsp sugar
¼ tsp salt

Method

- Fry in 3 tbsp oil the sliced shallots and garlic till slightly brown.
- Add in the curry leaves, green chilli, and *panch phoron* till fragrant. Set aside.
- Fry ingredients B – first the onion in 2 tbsp of oil, then add in the paste (remaining powders with some water) till fragrant.
- Add in the okra and fry well.
- Finally, add in fried ingredients A, stir fry, and serve.

6. Sri Lanka Eggplant

Further south in Sri Lanka, Mum and Pap spent some time in Galle, which is well known for its Portuguese architectural buildings and the Galle Fort. Initially occupied by the Portuguese, the Dutch later further fortified the fort. It is now a tourist trap with shops, museums, and some fine restaurants. Well known for their eggplant (or brinjal) curry dishes, this recipe came from another 'friendly' restaurant that serves it spicy and aromatic. The brinjal is marinated and deep-fried before it is immersed and cooked in a concoction of spices and coconut milk. Simply delightful.

Ingredients A

2 medium-sized eggplants, washed and cut in sticks
6 shallots, sliced
2 green chillies, sliced
4 tsp garlic paste
4 tsp ginger paste
½ tsp salt
1 tsp sugar
1 cinnamon stick, 2.5 cm long
4 cloves

Ingredients B

½ tsp turmeric powder
2 tsp ground mustard seeds
1 tsp chilli powder
2 tsp sambar powder
½ tsp of jeera (roasted cumin) powder

Ingredients C

½ tsp turmeric powder
¼ tsp salt
120 ml coconut milk

Method

- Wash, cut, and dry the eggplant, then rub ¼ tsp of salt and ½ tsp of turmeric powder.
- Deep-fry the eggplant till brown. Set aside.
- Fry in 3 tbsp oil the rest of ingredients A.
- Add some water to ingredients B to make a paste, then add in and continue frying till fragrant.
- Add in the fried eggplant.
- Finally, add in coconut milk and simmer till ingredients coat the eggplant. Serve.

7. Ayam Balado (Chicken Balado)

On one of their trips to Jakarta, the folks were invited to the home of Singaporean friends who had been living in Jakarta for over twenty years. The wife, a very good cook, was very keen in cooking Indonesian cuisine and had prepared a very sumptuous Indonesian meal. Her version of *ayam balado* was excellent and easy to prepare. She explained that the secret to a delicious plate of *ayam balado* lay in its paste. *Balado* is a fragrant chilli sambal made simply from a blend of shallots, chilli, garlic, and lime leaves. The term *balado* itself means 'with chilli' and can therefore be cooked with another ingredient, whether meat, seafood, or vegetable. The versatile sambal *balado* goes well with chicken, prawns, squid, boiled eggs, potatoes, eggplant, and even beef. Moderate the use of chilli for how hot or spicy you prefer your dishes to be. Again, as with most Asian dishes, this goes great with rice, or you may consider having it with bread or roti. All is good.

Ingredients A

1 kg chicken, cut in large chunks
2 tbsp garlic paste
1 tbsp vinegar
2 lime kaffir leaves
¼ tsp salt
½ tsp sugar

Ingredients B

3 cloves of garlic
12 fresh red chillies
100 g shallots

Method

- Marinate the chicken with the garlic paste and vinegar.
- Fry the chicken till brown. Set aside.
- Grind ingredients B preferably coarsely and fry in 3 tbsp oil till the oil breaks.
- Add salt, sugar, and lime leaves, then add in the chicken.
- Fry well, adding a little water. Simmer and serve.

8. Sambal *Goreng* (Spicy Fried Vegetables and Tofu)

Sambal *goreng* is a popular dish in Indonesia, Malaysia, and Singapore that Pap enjoyed, especially when it is included in a nasi Padang meal. Mum learnt this recipe from a food stall owner when they were visiting West Sumatra. Insisting that she take notes, the enthusiastic owner even handed her a pen and paper. His recipe for this protein-rich dish included green beans (Mum prefers French beans), tempeh, prawns, and boiled and cubed beef. We're not exactly sure why this dish is called sambal *goreng* as it means 'fried sambal' (chilli paste and spices) and does not describe the other vegetable and meat ingredients. What is true, though, is that all ingredients are fried separately before they are brought together with the sambal. And the final combination is a delicious, aromatic, and protein-rich side dish to go with rice or eaten on its own.

Ingredients A

300 g beef, boiled and cubed, 1 cm
4 packets of tempeh, cubed and fried
300 g French beans, sliced thinly and fried
120 g prawns, deshelled, cubed, and fried
2 tau kwa, *cubed and fried*
30 g assam *mixed with 60 ml water*
4 tbsp coconut cream
½ tsp sugar
¼ tsp salt
½ tbsp sambal belachan *(if not available, use 2 cm square piece of* belachan *mixed with 1 tbsp of dried chilli paste)*

Garnish

3 stalks of serai *(lemongrass)*
1½ cm ginger
8 cloves of garlic
3 fresh red chillies
1½ cm lengkuas *(blue ginger)*
6 shallots

Method

- Fry the sambal *belachan*, then add the sugar, salt, *assam* paste, and coconut cream.
- Add the beef, continue frying, then add the fried tempeh, French beans, prawns, and *tau kwa*. Stir evenly.
- Lastly, add in the garnish, all sliced thinly. Stir quickly, then turn off the fire.

No longer needing to support the kids, the folks travelled and spent more time eating out as there were fewer people at home to cook for. We were all busy with our careers, and my sister had moved to the United States. It was not until my kids came along when Pap got a chance to savour more of Mum's cooking. We always lived together, and my wife, Diane, and I agreed that it was good for the kids and their grandparents to experience one another's company. Interestingly, Pap was never strict with them as he was with us. He declared that bringing them up was our responsibility, and he was there to enjoy and spoil them. Still, we made sure the folks were never tied down, and the children grew close with them, benefiting from their love, wisdom, and learnings as well as good food. Looking back, it worked out very well for all.

On their eat-outs, the folks did experience their fair share of expensive fine-dining restaurants, but Pap was always about good food and to a large extent Asian food, regardless of the environment. It was also always about value for money. The next two dishes came from a reasonably priced restaurant that Pap liked and frequented in the '80s. The restaurant, since closed, is Xiang Man Lou at Bras Basah Complex. Their menu included tasty and somewhat common Chinese dishes, but the difference was in their innovation and tasty outcome. The folks liked the food there, so Mum befriended one of the proprietors who was previously a chef himself. He was quite generous and more than willing to impart his knowledge of foods and several recipes. In fact, Mum learnt a few tricks of the trade from him, for example, how to keep *bee hoon* springy and not break when frying or how to freshen/revive bean sprouts and keep them firm or how to maintain a nice crunchy consistency with prawns. All for another day. So here are the two recipes.

9. Crab *Tang Hoon* (Crab in Glass Vermicelli)

This crab *tang hoon* dish was a specialty at the restaurant. A popular dish best cooked and served in a clay pot, it can be found in many Chinese seafood restaurants as well as Thai restaurants. Where the difference lies in Xiang Man Lou's recipe is the use of satay sauce that brings forth a rich and peanuty flavour that enhances the overall taste of the dish.

Ingredients A

1 medium-sized crab, cleaned and chopped into 4 parts
1 packet of tang hoon *(250 g), soaked and strained*
120 g butter
4 cloves of garlic
1 fresh red chilli, sliced
8 shallots, sliced finely
¼ cup chopped cilantro
1 tbsp satay sauce
½ tbsp roughly ground black pepper
1 cup chicken stock
1 tsp dark soya sauce

Side Sauce

shredded young ginger in black vinegar

Method

- Dust the cut crab pieces with some cornflour. Deep-fry and set aside.
- Soak the tang hoon, then strain when soft.
- Fry the noodles in one cup of oil, then add in the satay sauce, black pepper, and chicken stock (enough to cover the noodles).
- Add the butter, whole cloves of garlic, sliced chilli, sliced shallots, and cilantro to the noodles and continue frying.
- Using a clay pot, place in the crabs and noodles and some chicken stock and bring to a boil for 10 minutes.
- Serve accompanied with shredded young ginger in black vinegar.

10. Fried Yong Tau Foo (Fried Stuffed Tofu)

The variation in this *yong tau foo* is really in frying the stuffed tofu and vegetables in a special sauce. A variety of fresh *yong tau foo* can be bought at markets or supermarkets. Frying and then braising it in the special sauce, followed by thickening the gravy with a cornstarch slurry, makes all the difference. It can be eaten on its own or accompanied with white rice.

Ingredients A

12 pieces of mixed yong tau foo, *scalded and drained*
1 piece of orange peel
1 star anise
4 tbsp water

Ingredients B

2 tsp chopped garlic
4 tsp chopped shallots
2 tsp tausi *(fermented black beans)*
2 tbsp sugar
1 tsp Knorr Hao Chi powder

Method

- Steam the orange peel and star anise in 4 tbsp water. Set aside.
- Fry ingredients B till fragrant.
- Add in the steamed ingredients and then the *yong tau foo* and continue frying.
- Lastly, thicken the sauce with a slurry of 1 tsp cornflour and some water.

11. Chai Boey (Mustard Greens Stew)

This recipe came from a well-known coffee shop serving Teochew porridge in Mosque Street, Chinatown. The folks frequented this eatery, especially when we were away at school as they were almost empty nesters at that point and were cooking less at home. Pap loved Teochew porridge, and Mum especially liked their *chai boey*. How she obtained the recipe is an interesting story. Apparently, the two brothers who owned the eatery were constantly bickering. On one of those occasions, they had a heated argument; and while still fuming, she boldly asked one of the brothers for this recipe. Surprisingly, he said, 'OK, but don't tell my brother I told you.' I guess this just demonstrates that timing is everything. *Chai boey* literally means 'vegetable leftovers'. This is not always the case in the eateries but is more commonly practised at home. It is often known for repurposing leftover meats; the preference is crispy roasted pork belly in the dish. The mustard greens, cooked till soft, is a simple, sweet, and sour stew that is comforting and incredibly easy to prepare. Crispy pork lard is used, which adds that extra flavour to the dish. Lovely!

Ingredients A

600 g salted vegetables (mustard greens), washed and boiled to remove salt
100 g pork lard, cut into small cubes and fried, retaining only the crispy parts
120 g roasted belly pork, sliced
3 cloves of garlic
3 tbsp sugar
¼ tsp garlic paste
¼ tsp fish sauce

Method

- After washing and boiling the salted vegetables, cut into small squares and again wash under running water. Strain and dry.
- In 3 tbsp oil, fry the garlic paste and the salted vegetables. Add the sugar, then set aside.
- Fry the whole cloves of garlic till slightly brown, then add the fried crispy pork lard and roasted belly pork.
- Add in the vegetables and the fish sauce. Season to taste.
- Transfer all into a Crockpot and cook for 3 hours till soft.
- Serve with porridge or rice.

12. Soto Ayam Istimewa (Special Chicken Soup)

Another favoured restaurant that the folks frequented was Tambuah Mas Indonesian Restaurant at Tanglin Shopping Centre. It is still there today and has also expanded with a couple of other branches. Mum really liked the *soto ayam istimewa* that was served there, but time and again, her charms failed to get the recipe. One day when getting a haircut at the same shopping centre a floor below the restaurant, she recognised that the lady washing her hair had previously worked at the restaurant. Apparently, she was a disgruntled employee who left the restaurant abruptly. Upon hearing this, Mum jumped at the opportunity to ask if she could get the recipe for her, and you guessed right – the lady delivered. The recipe is quite elaborate in its process but worth every effort. The mildly spicy soup is delicious and served with shredded chicken and beef, bean sprouts, *ketupat*, and *bergedil*. Garnishing includes fried shallots and cilantro. Truly outstanding.

Ingredients A

2.5 cm lengkuas *(blue ginger)*
2.5 cm ginger
2 stalks of serai *(lemongrass)*
3 cloves of garlic
15 shallots
6 buah keras *(candlenuts)*

Ingredients B

2 tbsp ketumbar *(coriander) powder*
2 tsp jintan manis *(fennel) powder*
2 tsp turmeric powder
1 tbsp black pepper

Ingredients C

6 tbsp oil
6 pieces star anise
25 cardamoms
10 cloves
1 cinnamon, 10 cm long

Ingredients D and Garnish

800 g chicken
450 g beef
2½ tsp sugar
3 tsp salt
fried shallots
½ cup cilantro
taugeh, *scalded*
ketupat
shredded chicken
shredded beef
bergedil

Side Sauce

5 chilli padi
3 cloves of garlic
2 tbsp lime juice
2 tbsp oil from the soup
1 tsp fish sauce
2 tbsp sugar

Method

- Boil the chicken and beef in 4½ litres of water for stock.
- When stock is ready, remove the chicken and beef, then shred. Set all aside.
- Grind ingredients A into a fine paste.
- Mix together powdered ingredients B with water to form a paste.
- Fry ingredients C in 6 tbsp oil till fragrant.
- Add in the ground paste and continue to fry till oil breaks.
- Add in the powdered spice paste and fry well.
- Pour in one-third of the stock and bring to a boil.
- Pour the entire mixture into the remainder of the stock and boil.
- Season with salt and sugar to taste. The soup is ready.
- Prepare the side sauce by pounding the chilli and garlic and then mixing with the other ingredients.

Finishing

- Place in a bowl or deep plate some rice cakes (*ketupat*), *taugeh*, and shredded chicken and beef. Pour the soup over generously and garnish with fried shallots, cilantro, and a teaspoon of the side sauce.
- Add a *bergedil* (recipe below) on top to complete a delightful meal.

13. Bergedil (Potato Cutlet)

Bergedil has often been mentioned as an accompaniment to several dishes such as *lontong*, mee *rebus*, nasi Padang, and *soto ayam*. This deep-fried potato cutlet can be found in many recipe books, and most have minced meat as an ingredient, mashed with potatoes and spices, and pan-fried. It is a superb accompaniment to a variety of noodle or soupy dishes, excellent when eaten with rice or even brilliant when served as finger food at parties or gatherings. Mum's *bergedil* comes with a little twist that makes a world of difference, and this was actually prompted by Pap. Instead of using minced meat, he suggested she use canned corned beef that is fried till dry. The corned beef adds a distinctive essence that makes the *bergedil* that much more flavourful.

Ingredients A

800 g Indonesian potatoes, boiled
60 g butter
60 g cakeflour
60 ml milk
1 egg yolk
1½ large onions, diced
½ tin of corned beef, fried till dry
¼ cup cilantro and spring onions, chopped
salt and pepper to taste

Ingredients B

1 egg white
100 g biscuit powder

Method

- Make a roux by melting the butter and then adding flour and cooking over low heat until thick and creamy/lump-free. Add the milk a little at a time until smooth. Cool and then whisk in the egg yolk. Set aside.
- Boil the potatoes. Peel when cooked, slice into fours, and lightly fry in 1 tbsp oil till slightly brown. Mash the potatoes when done. Set aside.
- Mix the onions, fried corned beef, cilantro, and spring onions and salt and pepper to taste.
- Work the roux into the mashed potato, then add in the corned beef mixture. Mix well.
- Shape into round cutlets and flatten.
- Beat the egg white and brush onto the patties, then roll the cutlets in the biscuit powder and shallow-fry till brown.

14. Babi Assam (Tamarind Pork)

This is a typical Peranakan recipe which Mum learnt from Mama Chit. For many years, she felt it was good but not great. Having tried a number of variations on the original recipe as well as other recipes, she was still not satisfied. There was something missing. Quite by chance one day after church, she was talking to a Eurasian man who boasted that his mother's *babi assam* was the best. She tried to pry the recipe from him, but he was extremely guarded. However, out of courtesy, he nonchalantly rambled off a few ingredients. Most were pretty standard, but Mum noted one that was not used in typical *babi assam* recipes. Using her mother's recipe, Mum added that extra ingredient, *taucheo*, and – voila! – it was the missing ingredient that made all the difference. At a church food fair some months later, Mum's contribution was *babi assam*. The same Eurasian man was there and tasted the dish. He immediately became annoyed, asking her where she got his mother's recipe from. Mum just smiled knowingly. She does, however, quietly credit his mother for that extra ingredient. It is amazing how just adding or taking away one ingredient can affect the overall quality and taste of a dish.

Ingredients A

1½ kg pork (½ pork belly and ½ shoulder butt)
350 g rempah assam *(refer to '*Basic Rempah *and Sauces')*
4 tbsp taucheo *(fermented brown bean paste)*
2 fresh whole green chillies
3 stalks of lemongrass, bruised
4 large onions, sliced
½ tsp dark soya sauce
35 g assam *paste (mixed with water)*
5 tsp sugar
1 cube of chicken seasoning
3 tsp ketumbar *(coriander) powder*

Method

- Cut the pork into bite sizes.
- Fry onions in 3 tbsp oil, then add in the *rempah*, *taucheo*, and bruised lemongrass stalks. Fry till the oil breaks.
- Add in the pork and fry evenly.
- Add the *ketumbar* powder, chicken cube, sugar, dark soya sauce, green chillies, and *assam* water. Mix well.
- Place all into a Crockpot and cook for 2–3 hours.
- Serve with white rice.

15. Babi Chinchalok (Pork Chinchalok)

This was originally a Filipino dish and is known as pork *binagoongan*. This recipe came from our Filipino domestic helper of twenty years. Belen was a qualified nurse who couldn't get a nursing job because of a speech impediment. A gentle and caring person, she cared for Pap, until he passed on, and the rest of the family when medical aid was required. Although she had very little cooking experience when she first arrived, by the third year after receiving much training from Mum, she became an excellent cook and started to gain a new passion. She was able to authentically produce Peranakan dishes and many of the recipes in this book, and her dream was to open a small eatery when she retired to her home in Tagaytay. On her twentieth year with us, Belen unfortunately developed breast cancer and had to have one breast removed. Having completed treatment here, she decided to go home to be with the family while we continued to support her treatment in Manila. She was, after all, family. Sadly, she had a relapse and passed away a couple of years after returning. We dedicate this recipe to Belen, who cooked it often as we all enjoyed it. Bagoong is the main ingredient, which is a Philippine condiment partially or completely made of either fermented fish (bagoong) or krill or shrimp paste (*alamang*) with salt. It is very similar to *chinchalok*, which is more easily available in Singapore. Bagoong can be bought in Lucky Plaza or online today. When it was not as easily available, Belen would substitute it with *chinchalok*. Hence, Mum calls the dish *babi chinchalok*, and the best cut used is pork belly. Served with white rice, it is yummy.

Ingredients

500 g pork belly, cut into 2.5 cm slices
2 tsp chopped garlic
2 large onions, sliced
3 fresh red chillies, chopped
2 tomatoes, chopped
3 tbsp sugar
1 tbsp vinegar
4 tbsp bagoong (or chinchalok*), rinsed under tap water to remove excess salt*

Method

- Blanch the pork and dry when done.
- Fry the onions, garlic, and chopped chillies in 3 tbsp oil till fragrant.
- Add in the chopped tomatoes and continue frying till tomatoes are mushy.
- Add in the pork, bagoong, vinegar, and sugar. Cook the pork till tender and dry.

16. Filipino Chicken and Coconut Broth

This is another Filipino dish Mum learnt from a Filipino lady friend who owned a restaurant in Makati. On one of their trips there, Mum found this soup so appetising that Vida, her friend, generously shared this recipe with her. Really simple to cook using aromatic ingredients, the addition of flesh from young coconut and Campbell's cream of chicken makes the broth rich and thick. The combination, especially the young coconut flesh with its gelatinous, jellylike meat and light flavour, adds a nice touch and body to the soup. Vida was adamant, though, that coconut juice should not be used as called for in similar recipes. This soup can be served as a starter or as one of several dishes when served Asian-style.

Ingredients A

500 g chicken thighs
200 g young coconut flesh
4 cm ginger, bruised
1 stalk of lemongrass, bruised
5 shallots, mashed
2 tomatoes, chopped
1 can Campbell's cream of chicken soup
1 can of water
salt and pepper to taste

Method

- Place the chicken, ginger, lemongrass, shallots, and water in a pot. Bring to a boil.
- When the meat is tender, add in the sliced coconut and the chicken soup.
- Add salt and pepper to taste.

LATER IN LIFE, DEATH, AND TODAY

Mum and Pap had a full life together. They were married for fifty-one years until Pap's passing in 2007 at 75 years of age. They travelled, ate, and kept each other company right to the very end of his life. They thoroughly enjoyed their time together, and theirs like many other similar marriages should indeed be an inspiration to all wedded couples. Going through the ups and downs of life's challenges, they stayed the course and stuck through it all together. Pap didn't always look after himself well; he had numerous health conditions, primarily hypertension, heart disease, and diabetes. During his career, he was consumed with work and the family, which didn't leave much time for exercise and hobbies. He did enjoy his drink, though, and that took its toll over the years. By the early 2000s, his knees were giving way and legs weakening such that he was wheelchair bound. Still, that didn't keep him down, and my parents spent much time on cruises, which were very good.

But being in and out of hospitals, I felt that perhaps the quality of life for him could have been better. In my opinion, he didn't retire as well as he could have, missing the life, attention, and glory days he had while in the police force. Perhaps it was the bane of that generation, whose focus was entirely on family and work. Having said that, it's not an 'old-fashioned' concept but a good one but just requires more balance. Having observed this first-hand at home every day, I have learnt that without hobbies, close friends, physical activity, and a good plan B, one can only watch that much TV or spend time in shopping centres or read. The frustrations do build up and will affect the temperament and people around you. As I am now in my retirement years, I have taken much of these learnings into consideration. The term *retirement* is defined as 'the time of life when one chooses (sometimes not of choice) to permanently leave the workforce'. It certainly does *not* mean retirement from life or productive activity as many choose to believe.

Being the traditional wife of an earlier generation who dedicated themselves to their men, Mum was always by his side and cared for him through all his illnesses. She would painstakingly learn about nutrition and healthy eating without compromising taste and quality as that would infuriate Pap. Using sugar substitutes and less salt, she would still produce tantalising dishes. She would attend dietary courses to learn how to manage his diet and eating. Pap had chronic diabetes, and Mum would administer his insulin every day and would not compromise on mealtimes and sugar management, especially alcohol, or at least she tried. Pap would on occasion cheekily steal a drink or two and have us or his grandsons collude with him. He wasn't exactly the easiest person to look after.

Mum also had a keen interest in medicines and would know exactly what drugs he needed and what would conflict, often challenging doctors when they prescribed the 'wrong' medicines due to the many conditions that he had. The family often joked that she was a quack doctor, but she did know her stuff, especially the side effects of drugs on him. Many doctors had complimented her for being the caregiver that she was and told her she probably extended Pap's life expectancy.

It was a strange but perhaps fortuitous ending for Pap. He was admitted into hospital for an infection and, partly due to his diabetic condition, went into a semi-coma state, somewhat unconscious and not responding to speech or sound. Mum stayed by his side all the while and slept on the couch in the room. I will never forget the experience while visiting him one day while still in his semi-coma state; he suddenly woke up and started to sing 'Danny Boy'. It was the weirdest experience. By this time, it was already a couple of months since he was admitted; and while in hospital, he was also diagnosed with cancer. In a discussion over this with Mum, the oncologist noticed Mum had a runny nose without any flu symptoms. Just to be safe, he suggested that she go for an examination and indeed found that she had an early-stage tumour behind her nasal passage. So both Mum and Pap had treatments together for another month or so. It was fortuitous as both were together in hospital, undergoing treatment and sharing the same room.

For Mum, her tumour was detected early. The treatments were effective; she has been in remission for over fifteen years now and considered cured. The only setback today is that she can no longer eat chilli or anything too spicy, very tough for someone who loved to eat and cook spicy food. Pap unfortunately did not recover and eventually succumbed to pneumonia instead. Mum was obviously devastated, even though she knew he was near his end when he was admitted. We arranged for the wake and funeral, and we were all shocked to see the throng of people who came to pay their respects, many Mum didn't even know. They were there because Pap had helped them in one way or another at some point in his life. Many of his old comrades and subordinates turned up to say goodbye, and it was indeed touching to witness many who saluted him before they left. One even organised for a bugler to play the last post at his funeral. They do say that the mark of a good man is demonstrated by who and how many people turn up at his funeral.

After the funeral activity, Mum was lost. She grieved and mourned quietly but was visibly shaken. For a change of environment, we took her away on a holiday in France, noting all the while her reminiscing of the places that she had been with Pap. The grandchildren were a blessing for her, and they took turns keeping her company. When we got back, Mum would remain much of her time alone, which we felt was not healthy. Belen, our loyal domestic helper, was a blessing as she kept Mum company most of the time. At that point, she had lost all interest in cooking and actually stopped for more than three years.

I give credit to my wife, Diane, who spent time with her trying to get her involved with church and other activities. The most successful of these was attending a 'tai chi for health' session at a community centre and then bringing Mum along to join the group. Mum took a liking to tai chi, which helped her with balance and exercise, and the class, which comprised students who were mostly retirees. She's even made friends with students younger than her children. She has persisted with these classes all these years, having found a nice social community in the class. I think tai chi has kept her healthy and active, and she practises every day without fail. Somewhat of a novelty for the class, she is the oldest student and remembers every step.

She finally got back to cooking when her grandsons kept pestering her to cook the dishes they missed over the three-year period. She admitted to being nervous and a little apprehensive when first getting back into the kitchen. Regardless, she didn't lose her touch. After a while, not only did she cook again many of our favourite recipes but she also started to experiment, improve, and innovate new recipes. Today she is a big fan of YouTube, still eagerly learning new methods and recipes and, typical of a Nyonya, criticising ones that don't meet her standards. Before Covid-19, she led a fairly active social life and even went out on her own. These last couple of years, Covid-19 has somewhat stifled her movements and social activity, but she has instead spent time cooking and passing on to me the finer points of her skills. This book has also kept her busy, and I will admit that it did surprise me that she has actively participated in its production.

So in this final chapter, we will share some of those newer creations and improvements from the past ten years or so. We hope you like them. We also hope that you found Mum and Pap's life and love story captivating and inspiring. It is Mum's ninetieth birthday, and her wish for all you home cooks is that you enjoy the recipes, feed your families, and maintain the culinary traditions that are so much a part of Singapore. After all, families that eat together stay together. This I have found to be true as my family of four boys and their better halves often get together at the dinner table over good food and wine, where conversations and laughter last till the wee hours. Mum penned a personal message to me in a book that she gave me as a present on my fifty-fifth birthday, in which she handwrote 222 recipes. I share this message as I believe it can be relevant to the readers.

> **Jay [what she calls me], I hope the recipes will inspire you to want to try them in the future. Treat cooking and baking as one of your hobbies, and you will derive great pleasure and satisfaction from them. I am certain that this book will serve you well in your retirement years. You can always gather the family to enjoy delicious and nostalgic meals and share many happy moments together.**
>
> **Enjoy!**

1. Hainanese-Peranakan Satay *Babi*

This delectable dish is somewhat of a fusion between the Peranakan satay *babi* and the skewered Hainanese pork satay. Both are excellent dishes on their own, but the combination produces a distinct flavour that is neither one nor the other specifically. I would like to think that it brings out the best in both. Really good!

Ingredients A

1 kg pork belly, 4 cm thick and cut into 1 cm slices
1 tbsp curry powder
½ tbsp chilli powder
½ tbsp garlic paste
½ tbsp turmeric powder
½ tbsp five-spice powder
1 tbsp coriander powder
2 tsp fish sauce
1 tsp ginger juice
1 tsp black pepper
3 tsp sugar
1 tsp salt

Ingredients B

60 g belachan
75 g roasted cashew nuts
5 shallots
1 tbsp sesame seeds
3 cloves of garlic
1 tsp chilli powder
1½ cm blue ginger
1 stalk of lemongrass
8 candlenuts
1½ cm turmeric

Ingredients C

½ tbsp curry powder
1 tbsp turmeric powder
¼ cup canned pineapple, pureed
½ cup canned pineapple cubes
250 ml pineapple juice
sugar and salt to taste

Method

- Marinade the pork with the rest of ingredients A overnight or at least 3 hours.
- Fry the marinated pork in shallow oil till fragrant. Set aside.
- Fry the finely ground ingredients B in 3 tbsp oil till the oil breaks.
- Add ½ tbsp curry powder and 1 tbsp turmeric powder.
- Add in the pork, ¼ can of pineapple puree, and sugar and salt to taste. Continue frying.
- Lastly, add in the pineapple chunks and the pineapple juice. Simmer until the pork is tender.

2. Mum's Mysore Fried Fish

Having tasted something similar in India, Mum came up with this recipe on her own. Using a mix of spices to marinate and remove the fishiness in the taste, the cubed fish, preferably white snapper or sea bream, is then carefully fried. With other ingredients and a complex mix of spices including *panch phoron* (the Indian five-spice blend), the outcome is a dry and delicious fish dish.

Ingredients (A)

600 g angkoli *(sea bream), cut in cubes*
1 tsp turmeric powder
1 tsp salt
2 tomatoes, chopped finely
1 large onion, chopped finely
2 shallots, sliced
2 cloves garlic, sliced
1 tbsp panch phoron *(Indian five-spice)*
1 tsp ginger paste
2 tsp garlic paste
¼ cup cilantro

Ingredients B

1 tbsp coriander powder
1 tsp chilli powder
½ tsp salt
½ tsp black pepper
½ tsp sugar
1 tbsp jeera (roasted cumin) powder

Method

- Marinate the fish with 1 tsp salt and 1 tsp turmeric powder.
- Fry the fish in 2 tbsp oil a little at a time to brown evenly and to prevent the fish from breaking up.
- Fry the sliced shallots and ginger with the *panch phoron* and set aside.
- Separately fry the chopped onion and tomatoes till a little crispy.
- Add in the ginger, garlic paste, and cilantro.
- Add in the fish and sprinkle in mixed ingredients B.
- Add the *panch phoron* mixture and fry till dry.

3. Tom Yam Spaghetti Salad

This unusual salad was inspired by the very popular Thai salads and Malay *kerabu* (salad). In fact, it is tom yam based, but Mum's recommended product, Tae-Pee instant tom yam paste, interestingly is Malaysian. She uses thin spaghetti or capellini, which is a nice fusion and makes the dish more delicate. If this is not available, then *bee hoon* can be used as a substitute. The spaghetti is initially fried with some ingredients, then cooled completely before mixing and tossed with the remainder of the ingredients. Simply delightful.

Ingredients A

500 g capellini, boiled with a pinch of salt, immersed for 5 minutes
140 g Tae-Pee tom yam paste
30 g brown taucheo
30 g dried prawns, toasted and chopped
30 ml lime juice
50 ml water
1 tbsp sugar

Ingredients B

100 g shallots, sliced finely
1 large onion, sliced
2 cucumbers, shredded
2 kaffir lime leaves, sliced finely
½ cup daun kesum *(laksa leaves), chopped*
½ cup mint leaves
1 tsp calamansi skin, sliced finely

Method

- Fry the tom yam paste and toasted dried prawns in 3 tbsp oil.
- Add the lime juice, sugar, and water, then add the capellini and fry well.
- Remove and place on a large platter to cool.
- When cool, add in ingredients B and mix in completely.

4. Piroshki à la Thermidor

Piroshki is a boat-shaped baked or fried yeast-leavened bun that comes with a variety of mostly meat fillings. Piroshki are a popular street food and comfort food in Russia which has spread across the world. They are yeast dough buns with a filling and are either baked or fried and can vary in shapes and sizes. Mum's recipe is a little different in that she uses crabmeat and calls it thermidor, which in fact is lobster cooked in a rich sauce. The crab replacement is less expensive (especially if you use crab stick, which is in fact imitation crabmeat) and makes a wonderful filling for the piroshki. Fried in oil, the buns are so crispy on the outside, yet the dough remains soft on the inside. Perfect for picnics, potlucks, or dinner at home where they are mostly served as a main course but often paired with a light soup or easy side salad. *Priyatnovo appetita!*

Ingredients for the Bread

400 g flour
50 g yeast
1 tbsp sugar
¼ cup water
¼ tsp salt
100 ml milk
2 eggs
50 g butter

Ingredients for the Filling

½ can of button mushrooms, diced
6 shallots, sliced
¼ can cream of mushroom soup
120 g cheddar cheese
1 tbsp sherry
2 tbsp evaporated milk
1 packet of surimi snow crab legs, sliced into three
2 stalks of spring onions, chopped

Ingredients for the Roux

85 g butter
85 g flour
3 tbsp chicken stock
3 tbsp milk

Method

- For the bread, mix ingredients A together and prove for 40 minutes.
- Make a roux by melting the butter, then add flour and cook over low heat until thick and lump-free. Add the milk a little at a time until smooth, then add the chicken stock and stir till smooth.
- For the filling, in 3 tbsp oil, fry the shallots, crab legs, and button mushrooms, then add the cream of mushroom, sherry, cheese, and the roux.
- Lastly, add the chopped spring onions and allow to cool to fill the piroshki.

Finishing

- Divide the dough into 16 balls, then flatten and fill with 1 tbsp filling.
- Fold the dough in half and pinch the edges and seal.
- Place the sealed edges facing downwards and set aside for 10 minutes.
- Deep-fry.

5. Black Sotong (Black Squid)

This dish was actually inspired by Pap, who was an armchair cook, but he had pretty good food ideas. Cut in rings and cooked using a range of ingredients and aromatics, it is delicious. Mum calls it black sotong (or squid) as the dish becomes black in colour due to sepia, which is the black/brown pigment derived from the ink sac of the squid. The ink is edible and is used to add flavour, and the taste of squid ranges from mild to rubbery. If cooked over medium heat, squid tends to have a mild flavour similar to that of shrimp and lobster. When overcooked, it becomes rubbery, which robs it and the dish of its unique taste. The general rule in cooking squid is to cook it briefly over high heat to keep it tender. Use a wok for a quick stir-fry. It is a lovely dish, but don't overcook the sotong.

Ingredients A

1 fresh red chilli
4 cloves of garlic
30 g belachan
5 shallots
1½ cm turmeric

Ingredients B

1 large onion, sliced
3 slices of blue ginger
1 stalk of lemongrass, bruised
salt and sugar to taste

Ingredients C

300 g squid, cut in rings
½ tsp pepper
¼ cup assam *juice*
1 tsp chicken seasoning powder

Method

- Grind ingredients A into a fine paste and fry in 3 tbsp oil until the oil breaks.
- Add in ingredients B and continue frying.
- Add the squid in and the rest of ingredients C. Stir-fry and serve.

6. Hor Pau (Pockets)

Mum calls this dish 'pockets' as it uses *tau pok* (tofu puffs) cut in half, grilled. and stuffed with goodies, synonymous with filling a pocket. Not so commonly found in eateries today, this is one of those recipes that Mum has worked to perfection. She uses tofu puffs rather than *tau kwa*, which is too heavy/meaty. The stuffing includes ingredients such as belly pork, fish cake, cubed boiled eggs, and cucumber and served with a special chilli sauce (found in 'Basic *Rempah* and Sauces'), which makes all the difference. It is excellent as a starter or finger food at parties or as a secondary dish accompanying mee *siam* or laksa.

Ingredients A

tau pok *(tofu puffs), 2 packets of 10 makes 20 pieces*
2½ slices of pork belly
2 tbsp dark soya sauce
2 slices of blue ginger
1 tbsp brown sugar
2 pieces of star anise
1 cinnamon stick (2 cm long)
150 ml water

Ingredients B

3 fish cakes, grilled and cubed
4 eggs, boiled and cubed
1 cucumber, centre removed and cubed

Method

- Slice the pockets in half, grill for 10 minutes, and set aside.
- In 2 tbsp oil, stir-fry the blue ginger, star anise, and cinnamon, then add the pork and brown sugar.
- Add in the water and put all into the Crockpot and cook for 1 hour.
- When cooked, remove and cut into small cubes.
- Mix the pork cubes with cubed ingredients B for the filling.
- Stuff the pockets (*hor pau*) and serve with *hor pau* chilli sauce (refer to no. 2 in 'Basic *Rempah* and Sauces').

7. Eggplant Pajeri

This eggplant dish has a sweet and sourish taste that is brilliant, even for those who are not big fans of eggplant, like me. The addition of cabbage and fresh pineapple is quite unusual and provides not just body but also flavour that breaks from the monotony of just eggplant. Simple in preparation, it is a healthy and nourishing dish that complements other dishes in an evening meal.

Ingredients A

2 tsp mustard seeds, pounded
2 tsp garlic paste
1 tsp ginger paste
8 shallots, sliced
2 tsp curry powder, made into a paste
3 whole dried chillies

Ingredients B

600 g eggplant (Chinese), quartered and cut in 3 cm lengths
400 g cabbage, cut in 2.5cm squares
200 g canned or fresh pineapple, sliced in 1.5 cm length
2 tbsp assam *water*
3 tbsp coconut cream
sugar and salt to taste

Method

- Marinate the eggplant with some salt and turmeric powder and fry in 1 tbsp oil. Set aside.
- Fry ingredients A in 3 tbsp oil till fragrant.
- Add in the coconut milk, *assam* water, and salt and sugar to taste.
- Add in the cabbage and pineapple and stir-fry.
- Lastly, add in the fried eggplant, stir-fry till combined, and then serve.

8. Stingray in Coconut Milk

Inspired by milky seafood soups that you find in Thai and Filipino cuisines, Mum adapted this simple recipe that can be cooked fairly quickly. She uses stingray, which is gaining popularity locally, especially barbecued stingray. The meat is firm and tastes good; the texture is similar to tuna but a bit more delicate when cooked. Tomatoes, cabbage, ginger, onions, vinegar, and of course coconut milk make for a tantalising broth that is super appetising.

Ingredients A

3 pieces of stingray, cut into 3 cm wide pieces
100 g cabbage, cut in 2.5 cm squares
1 large tomato, cut in wedges
1 large white onion, sliced
5 cm of ginger, bruised
300 g coconut milk
250 g water
3 tbsp white vinegar
sugar and salt to taste

Method

- Immerse the tomato, onion, and ginger in 250 g water.
- Add 3 tbsp vinegar, salt, and sugar and bring to a boil for 8 minutes.
- Add in the fish, cabbage, and coconut milk and continue boiling till cooked.

9. Tuna *Bergedil* (Tuna Potato Cutlet)

The ever-popular *bergedil*, which was shared in the 'Success and Abundance' section, contained corned beef. Here is another of Mum's creation that uses canned tuna. Great for those who prefer non-meat dishes, the tuna not only lends a delicious flavour but also combines well with the potatoes and other ingredients to produce a great accompaniment to other dishes or a very delectable finger food for parties.

Ingredients A

800 g potatoes (Indonesian is recommended), boiled
60 g butter
60 g cakeflour
60 ml milk
1 egg yolk
1½ large onions, chopped
2 tsp garlic, chopped
1 tin of tuna, washed, strained, and fried till crisp
1 packet of surimi snow crab legs, sliced into small pieces
½ can of button mushrooms, quartered
1 fresh green chilli, chopped
1 sprig of curry leaves
3 tbsp grated carrots
¼ cup cilantro, chopped
3 tbsp cheese
1½ tbsp fried shallots
1 tsp allspice powder

Ingredients B

1 egg white
100 g biscuit powder

Method

- Make a roux by melting the butter, then add flour and cook over low heat until thick and lump-free. Add the milk a little at a time until smooth. Cool, then whisk in the egg yolk. Set aside.
- Boil the potatoes. Peel when cooked, slice into fours, and lightly fry in 1 tbsp oil till slightly brown. Mash the potatoes when done. Set aside.
- In 2 tbsp oil, fry the garlic, chopped onion, and mushrooms, then add the crisply fried tuna, snow crab legs, and the remainder of ingredients A. Stir-fry quickly and remove to cool.
- Work the roux into the mashed potato, then add in the tuna mixture. Mix well.
- Shape into round patties and flatten.
- Beat the egg white and brush onto the cutlets, then roll the cutlets in the biscuit powder and shallow-fry till brown.

10. Malay Cabbage

A simple dish that is cooked Malay style, one that Mum concocted that goes great with a menu of spicy and chilli meat dishes. It's a nice vegetable accompaniment as it is mild and complements the spiciness with a slightly sourish flavour. Also, its yellowish hue due to the turmeric, looks great on the dinner table.

Ingredients A

2 shallots
2 slices of turmeric
4 cloves of garlic
3 slices of blue ginger
5 candlenuts
1 tsp dried prawns

Ingredients B

1 whole medium-sized cabbage, sliced about 1 cm thick
1 tomato, sliced in wedges
2 stalks of lemongrass, bruised
1 tbsp lime juice
½ tsp fish sauce
sugar and salt to taste

Method

- Grind ingredients A into a fine paste and fry in 3 tbsp oil until fragrant.
- Add in the cabbage, then all the ingredients B and continue frying till cooked.

11. Prawn or Crab *Ketumbar* (Coriander Prawns/Crab)

Mum formulated this dish that can be used for either prawns or crab. The main ingredient is coriander powder, but it also includes a bunch of other ingredients that add to the flavour and *rempah* for the prawns/crab. There is a hint of a curry flavour from the other spices and curry leaves, much like a dry curry that is highly complementary to the prawns or crab. Enjoy.

Ingredients A

1 kg prawns or crab, if preferred
5 shallots
1 tomato
4 cloves of garlic
1½ cm ginger
1 large onion
1 stalk of lemongrass
1½ cm turmeric
1½ cm blue ginger

Ingredients B

3 tbsp ketumbar *(coriander) powder*
1 tsp chilli powder
¼ tsp black pepper

Ingredients C

8 cloves
1 cinnamon stick, 5 cm long
6 cardamom
1 sprig of curry leaves

Method

- Slice ingredients A except prawns and fry till fragrant in 3 tbsp oil, then add ingredients C, followed by ingredients B.
- Add a little water or stock to moisten the fried ingredients.
- Add in the prawns (or pieces of crab) and fry till cooked and dry.
- Add salt and sugar to taste and a squeeze of lemon juice.

BASIC *REMPAH* AND SAUCES

What is rempah?

Rempah is a complex paste of spices used as the foundation of many Malay, Indonesian and Peranakan dishes. Properly prepared rempah is the backbone of cooking across the Malay Archipelago and Indonesia. It is the foundation of well-loved favourites from Beef Rendang to Peranakan Babi Pongteh. The literal meaning of the word is spice in Malay, but in practice a rempah refers to a paste of spices which imparts an intense flavour to a dish.

A huge diversity of ingredients may be deployed in a rempah. The most common denominators are chillies, garlic and shallots, but even the most basic of recipes will call for several more ingredients, such as turmeric, tamarind, and candlenuts. Specific recipes may contain a complicated litany of ingredients, but the aim is the same: to create the perfect harmony of flavours from ingredients that otherwise already taste bold on their own.

How to make it

Traditionalists demand that whole ingredients be pounded together using a mortar and pestle. It's backbreaking work that once served as a gauge of culinary prowess. This paste must then be fried over a gentle fire until it turns fragrant, and all the oil absorbed by the rempah exudes back out from it. Not doing so will result in a dish that tastes raw and unbalanced. Once the rempah has matured in the oil, vegetables, meat or fish can be added.

The science of rempah

Few people these days have any scruples about blitzing up a rempah in the blender, but the faster method is not more efficient. The blunt pressure of the pestle destroys the plant cell walls more thoroughly than blades, releasing more flavour compounds and forcing them to commingle. It also gives rise to a silky, unctuous texture, nothing like the pulpy product of a blender. Fibrous ingredients like the alliums, ginger-rhizomes and lemongrass stalks that are commonplace in rempahs benefit the most from the pounding process.

During the frying process these flavour compounds diffuse into the hot oil, which disperses them more thoroughly throughout the dish and over the tongue. Frying also dries up the rempah, concentrating the flavours - the apparent separation of the oil from the rempah indicates that no more water remains in the paste.

The above description of *rempah*, written by Stephanie Lim and taken from the Michelin Guide, is a clear and perfect description and definition of *rempah*. Traditional methods of pounding with a mortar and pestle do have the advantage of releasing flavours and improving textures of the *rempah*, but time is always of the essence. For time-constrained working mothers, for example, use the blender. It is a compromise that is certainly better than using ready-made packets of *rempah* from the grocery stores, but the outcome will still be authentic and the flavours intact.

We share two basic *rempah* recipes that is used in Peranakan cuisine. When meat, vegetable, or seafood is added to either of these two, they become complete recipes on their own. The addition of even more ingredients or spices to the basic *rempah* recipes results in more complex and sophisticated recipes. You will find both types in some of the recipes shared.

REMPAH

1. Rempah Titek (Basic Four)

We call this *rempah titek* or basic four, which on its own can be used for Peranakan satay *babi*, papaya *masak titek*, sambal *kangkong*, and many other recipes.

Ingredients

680 g shallots
55 g buah keras *(candlenuts)*
55 g dried chilli paste + 2 fresh red chillies
42 g belachan

Method

- Blend or pound the ingredients into a fine paste.
- Fry the paste in 3–4 tsp oil over a gentle fire until it turns fragrant, and all the oil absorbed by the *rempah* exudes back out from it.

2. Rempah Assam (Basic Seven)

We call this *rempah assam* or the basic seven, which again on its own can be used for rendang, Nyonya laksa, *babi assam*, *tulang babi*, and many other recipes.

Ingredients

680 g shallots
55 g buah keras *(candlenuts)*
55 g dried chilli paste + 2 fresh red chillies
110 g belachan
6 stalks of serai *(lemongrass)*
55 g lengkuas *(blue ginger)*
2.5 cm piece of kunyit *(turmeric)*

Method

- Blend or pound the ingredients into a fine paste.
- Fry the paste in 3–4 tsp of oil over a gentle fire until it turns fragrant, and all the oil absorbed by the *rempah* exudes back out from it.

Note: The basic seven is called *rempah assam*, but it does not include *assam* (tamarind) – another Peranakan mystery. However, in many dishes, *assam* is an added ingredient beyond the *rempah*, e.g. *babi assam* and *tulang babi*. Other ingredients could include coconut cream, *taucheo*, *ketumbar* powder, garlic, *bunga kantan*, and others.

SAUCES

No dish, whether Eastern or Western, is complete without an accompanying sauce, dip, or spread. Whether it be as simple as chilli *padi* in soya sauce or wasabi in Japanese soya sauce for sushi or even a steak sauce, sauces can make or break a dish. Here, we share some basic sauces that can accompany a variety of dishes to add zing and enhance the overall flavour of the dish.

1. Basic Chilli Sauce

This basic chilli sauce can be used for wonton mee, *bak chor* mee, *chwee kueh*, *soon kueh*, and many other dishes. It can also be used as the foundation for other chilli sauces.

Ingredients A

*200 g home-made dried chilli paste**
150 g bottled dried chilli paste (Sing Long brand works well)
1 small bottle of Koon Yick Wah Kee chilli sauce
½ tsp sar keong *(sand ginger)*
2 tsp vinegar
1 ½ tsp salt
115 g water
4 sng buay *(sour plums), soaked in water*
1 tsp sugar
4 tbsp oil
2 tsp light soya sauce
3 tbsp sesame oil

Ingredients B

4 buah keras *(candlenut)*
1¼ cm ginger
¾ tbsp garlic paste
2 shallots
¼ stalk of serai *(lemongrass)*
1¼ cm lengkuas *(blue ginger)*

Method

- Mix ingredients A.
- Grind ingredients B finely into a paste. Heat the wok with oil and fry.
- Add the mixed ingredients A and bring to a boil.
- When cool, pour into bottles and refrigerate.

*Remove the seeds and soak the dried chillies in water till they are rehydrated. Simply grind the chillies, and this is your home-made chilli paste.

2. Chilli Sauces for Specific Dishes

a. *Chwee kueh* – 2 tbsp basic chilli sauce + 1 tsp dried prawn powder
b. *Soon kueh* – 2 tbsp basic chilli sauce + 1 tsp sweet black flour sauce
c. *Hor pau* – 4/5 tbsp basic chilli sauce + 2 tsp black vinegar + 2 tsp plum sauce + ½ tsp garlic paste + 1 tsp dark soya sauce + 3 tsp sugar + 1 tsp light soya sauce + 200 ml water. Mix the sauces; add 2 cut green chillies, 1 finely chopped large onion, and cilantro.
d. Braised duck – 2 tbsp basic chilli sauce + ½ tbsp fried black *taucheo* + ½ tsp vinegar + a little water + a touch of sugar.

3. Chilli Sauce for Fried Foods and Fritters

Ingredients

300 g fresh red chillies
5 dried chillies
8 cloves of garlic
juice from 1 whole lemon
1 tbsp sugar
½ tsp salt
1 tsp oil
4 tbsp tomato sauce
water, depending on how concentrated or watery the dip is preferred

Method

- o Grind the chillies and garlic to a fine paste.
- o Add the remainder of the ingredients.
- o Bring the sauce to a boil and pour into bottles to store.

Note: This recipe is for quite a voluminous amount of chilli sauce, which can be kept in bottles and refrigerated.

4. Chilli Sauce for Steamboat

Ingredients A

60 ml basic chilli sauce (if not available, then 30 g chilli paste)
120 ml water
60 ml honey or malt
60 ml vinegar
60 ml plum sauce
¼ tsp fish sauce

Ingredients B

ground peanuts
chopped cilantro

Method

- Mix ingredients A and boil.
- Allow to cool and taste for sweetness and saltiness. Add a touch of sugar or salt according to preference.
- Add ground peanuts and plenty of cilantro.

5. Peking Duck Sauce

Ingredients

1 tbsp sesame oil
60 ml plum sauce
60 ml hoisin sauce
1 tsp five-spice powder
1 tbsp oyster sauce
a touch of water (optional)

Method

Mix all ingredients and serve.

6. Sauces for Vietnamese Spring Roll

A. 3 tbsp peanut butter + 2 tbsp hoisin sauce cooked in 150 ml coconut water and 100 ml soda or 100plus
B. 120 ml fish sauce + 300 ml vinegar or lime juice + 350 ml water + 40 g sugar. Mix and add sliced red chillies or chilli *padi*.

7. Sambal for Laksa

Ingredients A

100 g chilli paste
20 g dried prawns
40 g shallots
½ tbsp sugar

Method

Blend the shallots, chilli paste, sugar, and dried prawns and fry all till oil breaks.

8. Bengali Chilli Sauce

Ingredients

250 g fresh red chilli paste
6 cloves of garlic
30 g raisins, fried in ghee
1 tsp custard powder
120 ml tomato sauce
60 g sugar
120 ml vinegar
60 g sesame seeds
120 ml water

Method

- Blend all ingredients and cook to preferred consistency.
- Ideal as a dip for pakoras, *vada*, and accra.

RECIPE INDEX

Glossary

Translations are primarily for Baba Malay terms and names. Other non-Baba Malay terms will be highlighted.

Cultural Terms

ang pow. A gift of money packed into a red packet. Red is considered a symbol of luck, life, and happiness.

baba. A Peranakan male.

bibik. Form of address for an elderly Peranakan lady.

cherki. A popular card game originating from Malacca played by the Nyonyas of olden days. One needs to be familiar with the many Hokkien and Baba Malay terms used in the game.

Kristang. A creole language spoken by Portuguese Eurasians or Kristang or Serani, a community of people of mixed Portuguese and Malay ancestry chiefly in Malacca and to some extent in Singapore.

mak cik . 'Aunt' or 'auntie' in Malay.

Nyonya. A Peranakan female.

Parsi. Members of a group of followers in India of the Iranian prophet Zoroaster (or Zarathustra). The Parsees, whose name means 'Persians', descended from Persian Zoroastrians who immigrated to India to avoid religious persecution by Muslims. Today they are found around the world and have communities in over twenty countries including Singapore.

Peranakan. Has its origins from Indonesia or Malaysia and comes with multiple meanings. It means 'locally born' or the offspring of intermarriage between a local and a foreigner. In our context, *Peranakan* refers primarily to Straits-born Chinese – that is, to those born in the former Straits Settlements (specifically, Singapore, Penang, and Melaka) and their descendants, although some would also count the communities in Jakarta and Surabaya. The Baba and Nyonya culture or Chinese Peranakan culture is the mixture of the Chinese culture brought from China and the local culture in the Southeast Asian countries where the Chinese people settled, in addition to the influence of cultures from the European countries during colonisation. The culture in general evolved over 500 years within a matriarchal community.

pondok. A rough shelter, usually a crude hut or shanty, made from scraps of wood, cardboard, corrugated iron, etc.; loosely (often jokingly) a small house.

***sirih* box.** Various types of betel or *sirih* sets and receptacles were created in the Malay and Indonesian archipelago to hold the ingredients of the betel chew. A set generally comprises a receptacle for holding betel leaves, pots for areca, gambier, and lime and a nut cutter. A betel quid consists of a betel leaf smeared with lime, thin shavings of areca nut, gambier, and other ingredient such as cloves and tobacco, a wad of which would be rubbed against the teeth and gums after chewing betel.

Yahudi. Baba Malay for 'Jew'.

Food Terms

achar. Pickled spicy vegetables often served as an appetiser or an accompaniment to other dishes in different food cultures. Found across many Southeast Asian and South Asian countries, styles and ingredients vary, but the common factor is pickling.

assam. Tamarind. The juice from adding water to the pulp is often used in Peranakan and Malay cooking.

ayam. Chicken.

babi. Pork.

bee hoon. 'Rice vermicelli' in Hokkien.

belachan. A shrimp paste made from finely crushed shrimp/krill mixed with salt and then fermented. Used extensively in Peranakan and other cuisines across Southeast Asia.

bhindi. 'Okra' or 'ladies' fingers' in Hindi.

buah keras. Candlenuts.

bunga kantan. Torch ginger flower.

bunga telang. Butterfly pea flowers or blue pea vines.

chapati. Also known as roti, an unleavened flatbread originating from India and is a staple in many countries, especially in the Punjabi community.

chinchalok. A Malaccan food made from a type of small shrimp or krill called *geragau* (in Malay) fermented with rice and salt.

dahl. Red lentils.

dalcha. Indian lentil-based stew.

daun kesum. Vietnamese coriander.

daun limau purut. Kaffir lime leaf.

daun salam. Bay leaf (local).

fun. 'Rice' in Cantonese.

galangal/lengkuas. Blue ginger.

goreng. Fried.

haeko. *Petis udang* in Malay, a thick black paste made from prawns, flour, water, sugar, and salt. This thick black paste has a molasses-like consistency, an intense flavour, and a pungent smell, which is why it is usually diluted with warm water or other ingredients. It is used to flavour common local street foods like *popiah* spring rolls, Penang *asam* laksa, *chee cheong fun* rice rolls, and *rojak* salad.

hancur. Destroy or crush.

hong siew. *Hong* means 'red' in Cantonese, and *siew* means 'grilled/roasted'.

ikan bilis. Dried anchovies.

istimewa. Special or exceptional.

itek. Duck.

jeera. Roasted and ground cumin seeds in Hindi (dark brown in powdered form).

jintan manis. Fennel seeds.

jintan puteh. Cumin (light brown in powdered form).

kangkong. Water spinach.

keema. Minced/ground meat in Indian cookery, usually lamb or mutton.

keladi. Yam.

kelapa. Coconut.

kerisik. A thick paste made from dry-roasting shredded coconut until golden brown and then traditionally pounded in a mortar into a paste.

ketumbar. Coriander.

ketupat . Rice cake packed inside a diamond-shaped pouch made from woven palm leaf.

kiam chye. 'Salted mustard greens' in Hokkien.

kodok. Frog.

ku chai. 'Garlic chives' in Teochew.

kueh. Bite-sized snacks and desserts. In this context, Nyonya *kueh* is a part of the Peranakan tradition and food culture. It cuts across a multitude of puddings; sweet, savoury, or salty pastries; and cakes – many made with a rice or glutinous rice base.

kukus. Steam.

kunyit. Turmeric.

lam yee. A variety of preserved bean curd which is made with fermented red rice; it has a pungent aroma, salty in taste, and commonly used for marinating in Chinese cooking.

lap cheong. 'Chinese waxed sausages' in Cantonese.

lap yoke. 'Chinese cured pork belly' in Cantonese.

lemak. Generally used to mean rich, fatty, or flavourful; and in a culinary context, the term refers exclusively to the coconut milk's creaminess in dishes like nasi *lemak* and laksa *lemak* or Malay and Nyonya *kuehs*.

lengkuas/galangal. Blue ginger.

lontong. Compressed rice cake.

lor mai fun. 'Glutinous rice' in Cantonese.

manis. Sweet.

masak. Cook.

nanas. Pineapple.

nangka. Jackfruit.

nasi. Rice.

panch phoron. Literally means 'five spices' in Bengali. It is a spice blend commonly used in Eastern India and Bangladesh and consists of the following seeds: cumin, brown mustard, fenugreek, nigella, and fennel.

pangang. Roasted or grilled.

pati santan. Pure coconut milk that comes from the grated flesh of old coconut and pressed/squeezed without adding any water. This is the first squeeze and today can be substituted with coconut cream sold in cartons. The second squeeze is done by adding water to the same batch of grated coconut and is more diluted compared with the first squeeze.

pechah minyak. Roughly translated as oil breaking or oil splitting, it is a stir-frying process of properly and completely cooking the *rempah*. This paste must be fried over a gentle fire until it turns fragrant, and all the oil absorbed by the *rempah* exudes back out from it. It is a common term in Nyonya or Peranakan and Malay cooking.

pulut. Glutinous rice.

rebus. Boil.

rempah. A complex paste of spices used as the foundation of many Malay, Indonesian, and Peranakan dishes. Properly prepared *rempah* is the backbone of cooking across the Malay archipelago and Indonesia. The literal meaning of the word is 'spice' in Malay, but in practice, a *rempah* refers to a paste of spices which imparts an intense flavour to a dish.

sambal. A chilli sauce or paste typically made from a mixture of a variety of chilli peppers with shrimp paste, garlic, ginger, shallot, scallion, palm sugar, and lime juice. Sambals usually are served as hot and spicy condiments to accompany a variety of dishes. Sambal is also used as a spice paste, a marinade, and a dipping sauce.

sar keong. 'Sand ginger' in Cantonese.

sayur. Vegetables.

serai. Lemongrass.

seri kaya. Pandan-flavoured coconut and egg mixture that may come in the form of custard, jam, or spread.

serunding kelapa. Freshly grated coconut seasoned with spices and tamarind and then cooked (with no added oil) until it is dryish but still moist.

siew yoke. 'Roasted pork belly' in Cantonese.

sng buay. Sour plum' in Hokkien.

sotong. Squid or cuttlefish.

talam. Often used in a variety of Peranakan *kuehs* and means 'tray' or 'flat mould', mostly aluminium, that is used for steaming. The *kueh* is typically double layered often with glutinous rice as the base and a variety of toppings.

tang hoon. Glass noodles made from water and starch like mung bean starch, potato starch, tapioca, or green pea starch (Hokkien term).

taucheo. 'Salted, fermented brown soyaa beans' in Hokkien.

tau kwa. Firm tofu with a meaty texture that holds up well when deep-fried.

tau pok. Tofu puffs.

taugeh. Bean sprouts.

tausi. 'Fermented black beans' in Hokkien.

tempeh. A plant-based protein source that originated in Indonesia. It is made from fermented soyabeans that have been formed into a block and may include additional beans and grains.

tumis. Cooking style that involves frying with oil. Stir-fry or sauté.

tung kwa. 'Winter melon' in Cantonese.

udang. Prawns.

Acknowledgements

This book could not have been completed without the help and collaboration of the following people, to whom Mum and I are immensely grateful.

- My wife and best friend, Diane for the encouragement, initial editing whilst in Covid "detention", plating designs, selection of family photos, creating an art piece specially for the book, and shopping for groceries and ingredients.
- My good buddy of over 40 years, P. Ramakrishna, the former CEO of CIO Academy for penning the foreword. Rama who has himself published, is a close family friend and has enjoyed Mum's cooking often over the years.
- Alicia Yi, Vice Chairman and Senior Client Partner at Korn Ferry – a former colleague and good friend who seeded the idea of a mother-son collaboration project at a catch-up lunch shortly after my retirement.
- Justin Ong, professional photographer and best friend of my eldest son Christopher, for the many hours of patiently and beautifully capturing the dishes.
- Aiden F. Paguyan, our Filipino domestic helper who efficiently assisted with preparations and cleaning up our mess after cooking.
- My brother, Tony and sister, Daphne for their encouragement and inputs.
- Our sons and their better halves for their encouragement and enthusiasm – Christopher and Michelle, Brendan and Amelia, Adrian and Joette and Dominic and Fel.
- My many friends, ex-colleagues and golf buddies for their encouragement and support
- The team at Partridge Group – Alby, Jen, Kathy, Emman and Julius for their professional advice, smooth execution and encouragement during the process.

About the Author

Gerard (Gerry) Chai recently retired after four decades in industry and management consulting. He spent twenty-eight years with Korn Ferry, the world's leading executive search and global organisational consulting firm.

At Korn Ferry, Gerry was the country managing director for eighteen years and later chairman of the Singapore office. He was a member of the firm's global technology industry practice and led the firm's technology officers' practice in the Asia Pacific. He was also a member of the firm's board and CEO services practice. His earlier career was spent in sales with large technology companies.

Gerry holds a bachelor's degree in physics from McMaster University in Canada. He has also attended an executive management programme at Harvard Business School. For ten years, he was chairman of Enactus Singapore, a global non-profit organisation involving tertiary students focused on entrepreneurial action for social good. He is a fellow of the Singapore Institute of Directors.

Having retired in 2021, he remains active in the industry and is a mentor to senior executives and a board adviser to tech start-up companies.

Gerry has always been interested in cooking from his early days at university. A sometime cook ever since mainly due to the lack of time, he picked it up again with the onset of Covid-19 restrictions. Upon retirement, he has since been actively cooking at least three to four days a week, mostly trying out Mum's recipes and learning from her. He decided to write this book when an old colleague seeded the idea over lunch one day shortly after retirement. Apart from celebrating her ninetieth birthday and keeping Mum busy, active, and motivated, just the opportunity to work with Mum on this book will always be cherished.

Happily married with four adult sons, Gerry is an enthusiastic golfer and armchair football fan who enjoys cooking, eating, and music from yesteryear.

CPSIA information can be obtained
at www.ICGtesting.com
Printed in the USA
LVHW071044040323
740754LV00027B/359

9781543772746